THINK
YOU KNOW
IT ALL?

GENIUS EDITION

Also in the same series

Think You Know It All?
Think You're Mister Know It All?
Think You Know It All? History

DAN SMITH

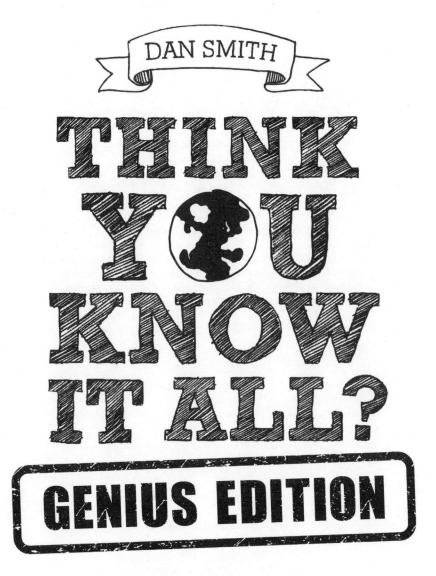

THINK YOU KNOW IT ALL?

GENIUS EDITION

THE ACTIVITY BOOK FOR GROWN-UPS

Michael O'Mara Books Limited

First published in Great Britain in 2021 by
Michael O'Mara Books Limited
9 Lion Yard
Tremadoc Road
London SW4 7NQ

A CIP catalogue record for this book is available from the British Library.

Papers used by Michael O'Mara Books Limited are natural, recyclable
products made from wood grown in sustainable forests. The manufacturing
processes conform to the environmental regulations of the country of origin.

ISBN: 978-1-78929-305-0

2 3 4 5 6 7 8 9 10

www.mombooks.com

Illustrations by David Woodroffe
Additional picture credits: Shutterstock

Cover design by Ana Bjezancevic
Designed and typeset by Allan Somerville

Printed in the UK by CPI Group (UK) Ltd,
Croydon, CR0 4YY

DEDICATION

For Matt, Amy, Will and Helena

INTRODUCTION

The *Think You Know It All* quiz books are not like other quiz books, which by and large use a scattergun approach to test your knowledge. Where other books test the *breadth* of your knowledge, *Think You Know It All* seeks to discover the *depth*. Rather than asking, say, which novelist wrote a novel featuring Cathy and Heathcliff, it instead demands to know the complete works of Emily Brontë. It's a format with no hiding place and is great for exposing the vanity of the know-it-all in your life! (By the way, if you think you don't know a know-it-all, it'd be best to double-check that it's not you.)

This, then, is the **Genius Edition** – the most challenging in the series so far but imbued with the same DNA. *Think You Know It All With Knobs On*, as my grandmother might have called it. The subject matter is wide – from science and nature, geography, history and politics to literature, film, music, art, sport and much else besides. There is a mix of quiz types, too: from the classic 'complete the list' to picture rounds, anagrams, mind-bending dingbats and a wordsearch with a difference. One minute you'll be trying to remember all the World Cup Golden Boot winners, the next you'll be mulling over the career opus of Harrison Ford or labelling a map of Italy's regions.

This book does not pretend to be anything other than tough.
We don't want you to rattle through these quizzes in a couple of minutes
each. Where's the fun in that?! Instead, they are designed to occupy
your mind for much longer. The pay-off is that while most quizzes urge
competitiveness, this book actively encourages co-operation.

We have all suffered family get-togethers ruined by Great-Uncle
Geoff (or someone similar) unleashing their unattractive desire to best
everyone else when it comes to trivia. But I defy anyone to carry around
in their head all the knowledge required to complete these challenges.
The real joy is to be had by pooling knowledge – exchanging your
knowledge of, say, single-term US Presidents for your niece's uncanny
recollection of the Harry Potter horcruxes.

And if the solutions sometimes elude you altogether, no problem.
The answers are all tucked away at the back. So, sit back, relax and throw
yourself into a mental workout like no other. And don't be tempted to
rush. As the self-styled 'genius' Gertrude Stein noted: 'It takes a lot of
time to be a genius. You have to sit around so much, doing nothing,
really doing nothing.'

SO ... THINK YOU MIGHT BE A GENIUS ?

A River Runs Through It

The River Nile runs through or along the border of
which eleven countries?

Name the Author

Who wrote the following works of a scientific and/or
environmentalist bent?

A.   *The Voyage of the Beagle*

B.   *Relativity: The Special and General Theory*

C.   *The Selfish Gene*

D.   *The Cosmic Connection*

E.   *Silent Spring*

F.   *Gorillas in the Mist*

G.   *Gaia*

Answers on page 152

Keeping Composed

Who wrote the musical scores for these famous shows?

A. *Porgy and Bess*

B. *Waitress*

C. *Sunset Boulevard*

D. *Hamilton*

E. *Little Shop of Horrors*

F. *A Little Night Music*

G. *Miss Saigon*

H. *The Rocky Horror Show*

I. *Cabaret*

J. *The Sound of Music*

Answers on page 152

Border Checks Part I

Can you identify the countries from these outlines?

A.

B.

C.

D.

E.

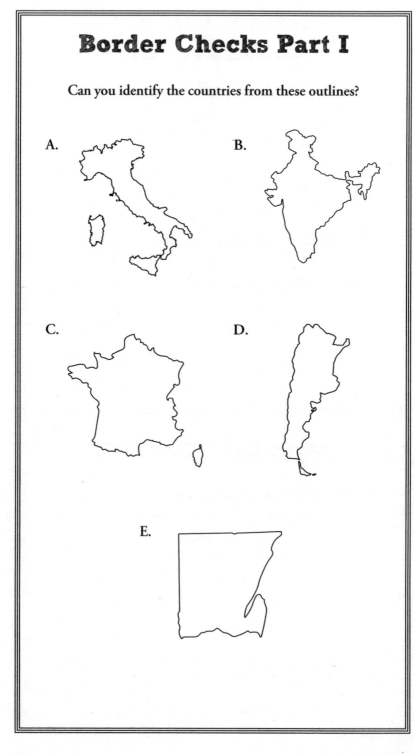

Answers on page 153

Taste Sensations

What are the five basic flavours that humans can sense?

1.

2.

3.

4.

5.

Lend Me Your Ears

In Mark Antony's famous speech in Shakespeare's *Julius Caesar*, whom did he ask to lend him their ears?

Answers on page 154

South American States

South America is traditionally considered to include which twelve sovereign states?

Moons of the Solar System

What are the names of the seven largest moons in the solar system?

Answers on page 154

Bond Theme Songs

The James Bond franchise is almost as famous for its theme songs as the movies themselves. Can you identify the artist who performed each of the following Bond songs?

A. 'Thunderball'

B. 'Live and Let Die'

C. 'The Man with the Golden Gun'

D. 'Nobody Does it Better' (for *The Spy Who Loved Me*)

E. 'Moonraker'

F. 'For Your Eyes Only'

G. 'All Time High' (for *Octopussy*)

H. 'A View to a Kill'

I. 'The Living Daylights'

J. 'Licence to Kill'

K. 'GoldenEye'

L. 'Tomorrow Never Dies'

M. 'The World Is Not Enough'

N. 'Die Another Day'

O. 'You Know My Name' (for *Casino Royale*)

P. 'Another Way to Die' (for *Quantum of Solace*)

Q. 'Skyfall'

R. 'Writing's on the Wall' (for *Spectre*)

S. 'No Time to Die'

Answers on pages 154–155

The Horcrux of the Matter

In the Harry Potter novels, what were Lord Voldemort's seven horcruxes (an object that contains a fragment of soul)?

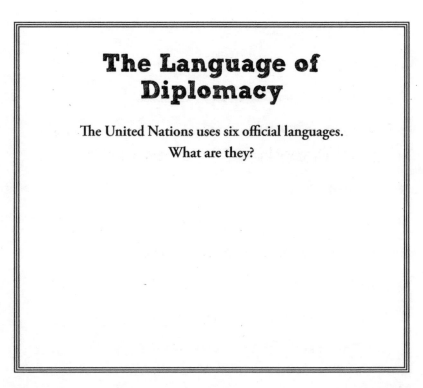

The Language of Diplomacy

The United Nations uses six official languages. What are they?

Answers on page 155

Premier League Champions

Since its foundation in 1992, seven clubs have won the
English Premier League soccer title (as of 2020).
Can you name them all?

In Vogue

In her classic hit, 'Vogue', Madonna namechecks sixteen
Hollywood legends. Can you name them all?

Answers on page 155

International Leaders Part I

How well do you know your international politics?
Can you name the five global figures pictured below?

A.

B.

C.

D.

E.

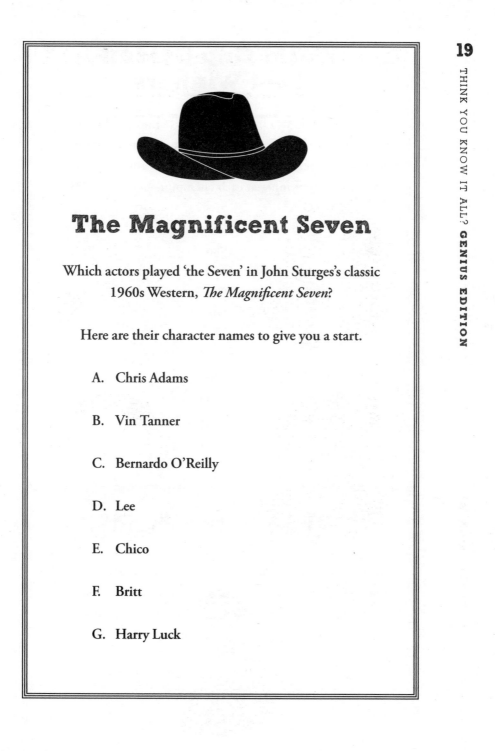

The Magnificent Seven

Which actors played 'the Seven' in John Sturges's classic 1960s Western, *The Magnificent Seven*?

Here are their character names to give you a start.

A. Chris Adams

B. Vin Tanner

C. Bernardo O'Reilly

D. Lee

E. Chico

F. Britt

G. Harry Luck

Answers on page 156

World Cup Golden Boot Winners

At every FIFA World Cup since 1982, the tournament's leading goalscorer has received the Golden Boot (or, until 2006, a shoe). Who was the winner at each championship up to 2018?

1982

1986

1990

1994

1998

2002

2006

2010

2014

2018

Who's in the Band?

Can you name the classic line-ups of three superstar bands who dominated the charts in the 1980s and 1990s — New Kids on the Block, The Spice Girls, and Destiny's Child?

Answer on page 156

Currencies of the World

Can you identify the currency used in each of the following countries?

A. Afghanistan

B. Belarus

C. Bolivia

D. Czechia

E. Denmark

F. Gambia

G. Hungary

H. Iraq

I. Israel

J. Kenya

K. Malaysia

L. Mauritius

M. Morocco

N. Nicaragua

O. North Korea

P. Poland

Q. Qatar

R. Thailand

S. Turkey

T. Vietnam

Answer on page 157

Volcanoes

According to the Smithsonian's National Museum of Natural History's Global Volcanism Program, which are the ten countries with the most active volcanoes?

Sherlock Holmes Novels

Arthur Conan Doyle wrote four full-length Sherlock Holmes books (and fifty-six short stories), but can you name them?

Answers on page 157

The Kentucky Derby

Below are the names of five legendary winners of the Kentucky Derby and two entirely fictional horses. Can you spot the pair of imposters?

Lincoln's Cigar

American Pharaoh

Seattle Slew

Citation

Startled Charlie

Spectacular Bid

Secretariat

Screen Legend

Which Hollywood giant has been portrayed on screen by Anthony Hopkins (2012), Toby Jones (2012) and Roger Ashton-Griffiths (2014)?

Answers on page 157

Spot the Landmark

Here are the silhouettes of some famous landmarks, but what are
they and in which cities are they located?

A

F

B

G

C

H

D

I

E

J

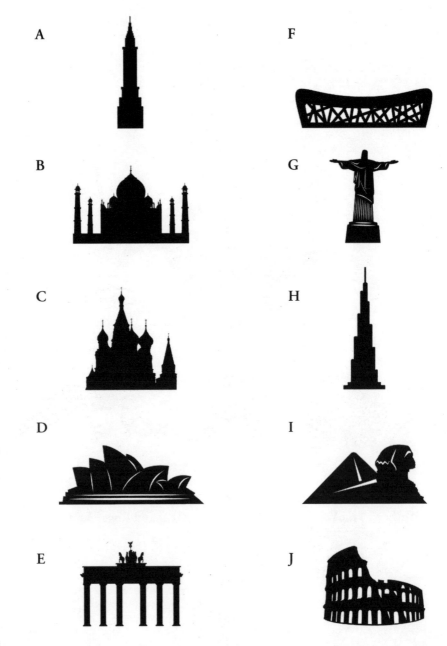

Answers on page 158

Which Witch is Which?

Can you name the famous witches and wizards from the visual clues?

A

B

C

D

E

Answer on page 159

In the words of POTUS Part I

It is a well-trodden path for those who ascend to the presidency of the United States of America to tell their side of the story. Here are the titles of six autobiographical works by former Presidents. But which of them wrote which?

A. *Keeping Faith: Memoirs of a President*
B. *At Ease: Stories I Tell to Friends*
C. *My Life*
D. *A Time to Heal*
E. *Surviving at the Top*
F. *Decision Points*

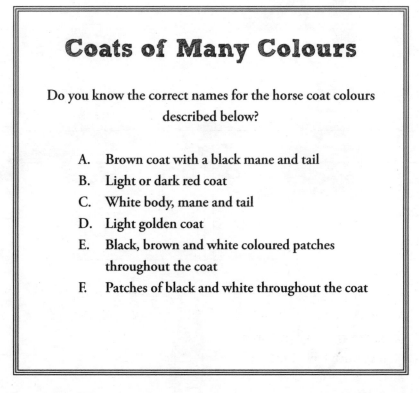

Coats of Many Colours

Do you know the correct names for the horse coat colours described below?

A. Brown coat with a black mane and tail
B. Light or dark red coat
C. White body, mane and tail
D. Light golden coat
E. Black, brown and white coloured patches throughout the coat
F. Patches of black and white throughout the coat

Those Magnificent Men in Their Flying Machines

Match the aviation pioneers to the historic journeys shown on the map.

A.

C.

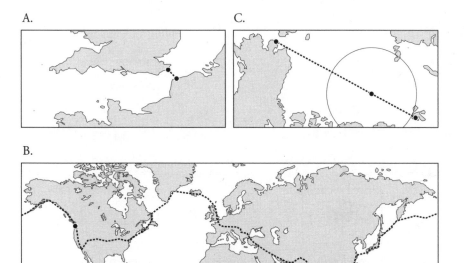

B.

D.

E.

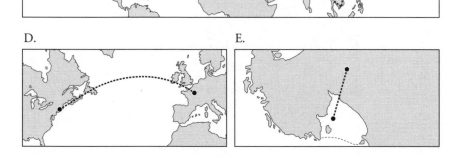

A. Calais to Dover, 1909

B. Seattle to Seattle, 1924

C. Spitzbergen to Teller, over the North Pole, 1926

D. New York to Paris, 1927

E. Ross ice shelf, 1929

Answers on page 159

Flags

What are the colours of the following national flags?

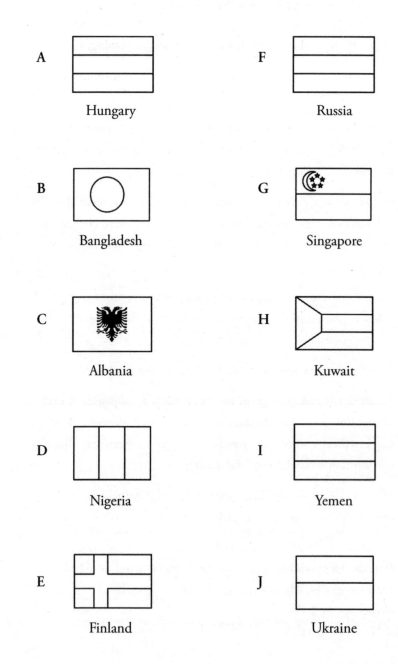

A — Hungary

B — Bangladesh

C — Albania

D — Nigeria

E — Finland

F — Russia

G — Singapore

H — Kuwait

I — Yemen

J — Ukraine

Answers on page 159

Shakespeare's Opening Lines

Here are the openings of ten Shakespeare plays.
Can you match the lines to the play?

A. 'When shall we three meet again? In thunder, lightning, or in rain?'

B. 'Now is the winter of our discontent made glorious summer by this son of York.'

C. 'O for a muse of fire, that would ascend the brightest heaven of invention: a kingdom for a stage, princes to act, and monarchs to behold the swelling scene!'

D. 'As I remember, Adam, it was upon this fashion bequeathed me by will but poor a thousand crowns, and, as thou sayest, charged my brother, on his blessing, to breed me well – and there begins my sadness.'

E. 'So shaken as we are, so wan with care, find we a time for frighted peace to pant, and breathe short-winded accents of new broils to be commenced in strands afar remote.'

F. 'In delivering my son from me, I bury a second husband.'

G. 'Noble patricians, patrons of my right, defend the justice of my cause with arms. And countrymen, my loving followers, plead my successive title with your swords. I am his first-born son, that was the last that wore the imperial diadem of Rome.'

H. 'If music be the food of love, play on; give me excess of it that, surfeiting, the appetite may sicken, and so die.'

I. 'Two households, both alike in dignity in fair Verona, where we lay our scene, from ancient grudge break to new mutiny, where civil blood makes civil hands unclean.'

J. 'Nay, but this dotage of our General's o'erflows the measure.'

Answers on page 160

All Roman to Me

By what names were the following modern nations known by the Romans (sometimes as part of geographically larger territories):

A. France

B. Tunisia

C. Romania

D. Switzerland

E. Ireland

F. Spain

G. Lebanon

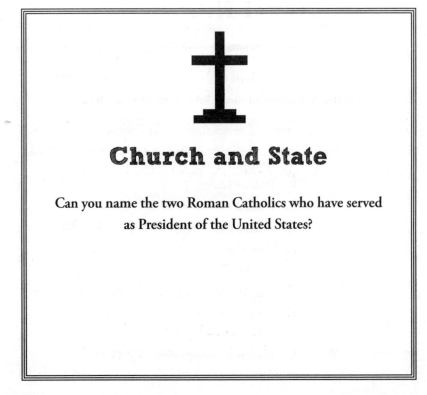

Church and State

Can you name the two Roman Catholics who have served as President of the United States?

Answers on page 160

Champs

All but two of these drivers won the Formula 1 motor racing title.
Who were the two who came close but never took the top spot?

Alberto Ascari
Gerhard Berger
Jack Brabham
Mike Hawthorn
Stirling Moss
Keke Rosberg
Jody Scheckter
Jacques Villeneuve

Novel Numbers

Below are listed ten authors who, in the year indicated, each
published a renowned novel with a number in the title.
Can you name each of the works?

A. George Orwell (1949)

B. Helene Hanff (1970)

C. Khaled Hosseini (2007)

D. Agatha Christie (1927)

E. Jules Verne (1872)

F. Ray Bradbury (1953)

G. Gabriel García Márquez (1967)

H. Kurt Vonnegut Jr (1969)

I. Mitch Albom (2003)

J. Nathaniel Hawthorne (1851)

Answers on page 160

SI Prefixes

———◆◆◆———

In the SI system of measurements, the addition of the prefix kilo denotes multiplication by a thousand. But what are the prefixes that denote the following multiplication factors?

A. 1,000,000

B. 1,000,000,000

C. 1,000,000,000,000

D. 1,000,000,000,000,000

E. 1,000,000,000,000,000,000

F. 1,000,000,000,000,000,000,000

G. 1,000,000,000,000,000,000,000,000

Beatles US No. 1s

The Beatles achieved twenty No. 1 hits on the US Billboard chart but can you name them all?

Sports Grounds

At which famous palaces of sport do the following teams play?

A. Boston Red Sox

B. Glasgow Rangers

C. River Plate

D. AC / Inter Milan

E. Flamengo (and frequently, the
Brazilian national football team)

F. Real Madrid

G. New York Knicks

H. Chicago Cubs

I. Brisbane Lions

J. Kaizer Chiefs

Answers on page 161

Who was Who in Game of Thrones?

Can you name the characters played by the actors below
in the *Game of Thrones* television series?

    A. Natalie Dormer

    B. Mark Addy

    C. Nikolaj Coster-Waldau

    D. Emilia Clarke

    E. Sean Bean

    F. Iain Glen

    G. Maisie Williams

    H. Alfie Allen

    I. James Cosmo

    J. Charles Dance

Answers on page 161

Papal Names

The Pope is, of course, the head of the Roman Catholic Church.
Here are the birth names of eight relatively recent popes, but what are
their papal names?

    A. Karol Józef Wojtyła

    B. Giovanni Battista Enrico Antonio Maria Montini

    C. Joseph Aloisius Ratzinger

    D. Achille Ambrogio Damiano Ratti

    E. Eugenio Maria Giuseppe Giovanni Pacelli

    F. Angelo Giuseppe Roncalli

    G. Jorge Mario Bergoglio

    H. Albino Luciani

Answers on page 163

Border Checks Part II

Can you identify the countries from these outlines?

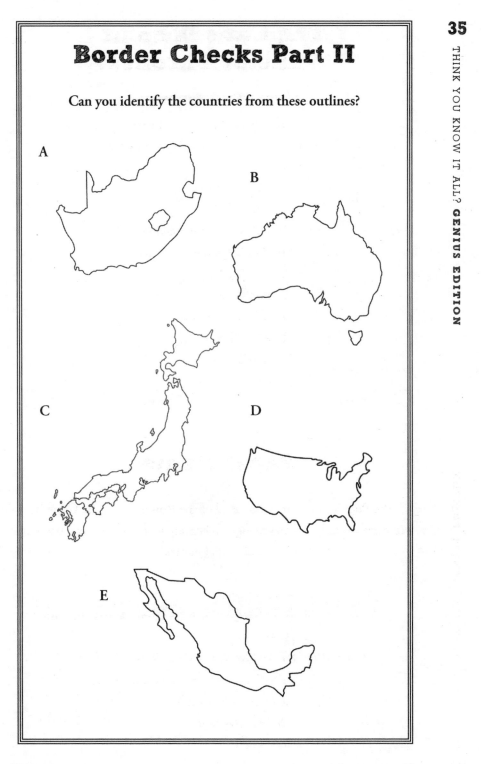

A

B

C

D

E

The Car's the Star

Which firms make (or made) the following famous car models?

A. Sprite

B. Passat

C. Eldorado

D. 2CV

E. Midget

F. MX-5

G. Panda

H. Accord

I. Celica

J. E-type

K. Micra

L. Cherokee

M. Elise

N. GranTurismo

O. Sierra

P. 911

Q. Spider

R. Viper

S. Lancer

T. Riviera

I Like to Ride My Bicycle

Which three races make up cycling's Grand Tour series?

Answers on page 163

Dingbats Part I

Can you decipher the famous names from the visual clues below?

A.

B.

C.

Answers on page 163

The Animals of Beatrix Potter

Beatrix Potter inhabited her world with a magical cast of creatures. Here are a dozen of them, but do you know what sort of animal each one is?

A. Mrs Tiggy-Winkle

B. Tommy Brock

C. Mr Jeremy Fisher

D. Mr Jackson

E. Mr Tod

F. Diggory Diggory Delvet

G. Tabitha Twitchit

H. Timmy Tiptoes

I. Hunca Munca

J. Samuel Whiskers

K. Cecily Parsley

L. Aunt Pettitoes

Raffle Winner

With which drink is the Raffles Hotel particularly associated, it having been invented there?

Answers on pages 163–4

On Brand

Brand names can become so familiar that we scarcely give a thought to what they might actually mean. Here are a few clues to the etymological origins of some global brands.
Can you work out which each one is?

A. The ancient Greek goddess of Victory

B. Korean for 'three stars'

C. Korean for 'modernity'

D. Derived from the Latin for 'snow white'

E. Named after a South African antelope

F. German for 'master of hunters'

G. Danish for 'play well'

H. German for 'people's car'

I. Named after company founder Adolf Dassler

J. An acronym of the Dutch phrase that means 'Through united co-operation everyone regularly profits'

K. Latin for 'I roll'

Answers on page 164

International Leaders Part II

How well do you know your international politics?
Can you name the five global figures pictured below?

A.

B.

C.

D.

E.

Answers on page 164

Reigning Monarchs

As of 2021, of which countries are each of the following monarchs head of state?

A. Philippe

B. Salman bin Abdulaziz

C. Carl XVI Gustaf

D. Jigme Khesar Namgyel Wangchuck

E. Hans-Adam II

F. Harald V

G. Tupou VI

H. Felipe VI

I. Norodom Sihamoni

J. Abdullah II

K. Prince Albert II

L. Letsie III

M. Margrethe II

N. Mohammed VI

O. Willem-Alexander

Colourful Stories

Below are the titles of ten celebrated works of fiction each with colours somewhere in their title. But who wrote them?

A. *The Scarlet Letter*

B. *Half of a Yellow Sun*

C. *The Green Mile*

D. *A Clockwork Orange*

E. *The Amber Spyglass*

F. *The Bluest Eye*

G. *The Color Purple*

H. *Black Beauty*

I. *The White Tiger*

J. *Fifty Shades of Grey*

Answers on pages 164–5

The Regions of Italy

Can you label the map below to show the twenty regions of Italy?

A Sporting Chance

In which sports do each of the following teams compete?

A. Arizona Coyotes

B. Sydney Swans

C. St Louis Cardinals

D. Kolkata Knight Riders

E. Catalan Giants

F. Toronto Raptors

G. Metalist Kharkiv

H. Carolina Panthers

I. Sale Sharks

Answers on pages 165–6

Poetry to My Ears

Can you identify the poet who penned the following famous lines of verse?

A. 'To err is human; to forgive, divine'

B. 'Look on my works, ye mighty, and despair'

C. 'Because I could not stop for death / He kindly stopped for me'

D. 'Tread softly because you tread on my dreams'

E. 'The time has come', the Walrus said, / 'To talk of many things'

F. 'The child is father of the man'

G. ''Tis better to have loved and lost / Than never to have loved at all'

H. 'Rose is a rose is a rose is a rose'

I. 'I am the master of my fate'

J. 'Candy / Is dandy / But liquor / Is quicker'

K. 'In Flanders fields the poppies blow'

L. 'Beauty is truth, truth beauty; that is all'

M. 'Dying is an art, like everything else'

N. 'I grow old . . . I grow old . . . / I shall wear the bottoms of my trousers rolled'

O. 'Stop all the clocks, cut off the telephone'

P. 'You declare you see me dimly / through a glass which will not shine'

Q. 'Do not go gentle into that good night, / Old age should burn and rave at close of day'

R. 'Two roads diverged in a yellow wood'

S. 'In Xanadu did Kubla Khan / A stately pleasure-dome decree'

T. 'How do I love thee? Let me count the ways'

Answers on page 166

The Need for Speed

In which countries would you find these famous motor racing circuits?

A. Calder Park

B. Paul Ricard

C. Imola

D. Hockenheimring

E. Autodromo Hermanos Rodriguez

F. Red Bull Ring

G. Sonoma

H. Suzuka

I. Estoril

J. Autodromo Juan Y Oscar Galvez

K. Sepang

L. Kyalami

M. Zandvoort

N. Circuit Gilles Villeneuve

O. Interlagos

P. Spa Francorchamps

Animal Art

George Stubbs is best known for painting which animals?

Answers on pages 166–7

Acting Out

The following performers all received Best Actor Oscars for
playing real people. But who did each impersonate?

A. Rami Malek

B. Marion Cotillard

C. Reese Witherspoon

D. Jamie Foxx

E. Gary Oldman

F. Olivia Colman

G. Daniel Day-Lewis

H. Meryl Streep

I. Colin Firth

J. Sean Penn

K. Forest Whitaker

L. Helen Mirren

M. Philip Seymour Hoffman

N. Nicole Kidman

O. Marcia Gay Harden

P. Eddie Redmayne

Q. Julia Roberts

Up to the Ockey

Can you remember where each of the numbers 1 to 20 go on
a standard dart board?

Answers on page 167

A Rose by Any Other Name

Listed are the real names of some of the biggest figures in the world of entertainment. But how are they better known?

A. Vincent Damon Furnier

B. Maurice Joseph Micklewhite, Jr

C. Marion Mitchell Morrison

D. Saul Hudson

E. Onika Tanya Maraj

F. Katheryn Elizabeth Hudson

G. Alecia Moore

H. David Evans

I. Helen Folasade Adu

J. Curtis James Jackson III

K. Cordozar Calvin Broadus

L. Alicia Augello Cook

M. Eilleen Regina Edwards

N. James Todd Smith

O. James Newell Osterberg, Jr

P. Elizabeth Woolridge Grant

All Hail the Braille

Do you know how to form the twenty-six letters of the alphabet using the six-dot system of Braille?

Off the Scale

What are measured by the following?

A. Micromort
B. Centipawn
C. Glasgow scale
D. Ohm
E. Scoville scale

F. Big Mac index
G. Hands
H. Candela
I. Mole
J. Kelvin

Name That Tunesmith

With which composers are these musical works most famously associated?

A. 'Nessun dorma'

B. *Peer Gynt*

C. *The Four Seasons*

D. 'Adagio for Strings'

E. 'Ride of the Valkyries'

F. 'O Fortuna'

G. 'The Planets'

H. 'On the Beautiful Blue Danube'

I. 'Pathétique'

J. 'Habanera'

K. 'Eine Kleine Nachtmusik'

L. *The Barber of Seville*

M. *Má Vlast (My Fatherland)*

N. 'Hallelujah Chorus'

O. 'Pavane'

P. 'Radetzky March'

Q. *Egmont*

R. 'Vocalise'

Answers on page 169

Mona Lisa

Here are a few teasers to test your knowledge of, arguably, the most famous work of art in the world, the *Mona Lisa*.

A. Who painted this picture?

B. By what alternative Italian name is the picture known

C. Who is thought to be the model for the painting?

D. Who had the painting hanging in their bathroom at the Tuileries Palace?

E. Where does it hang today?

F. How is Vincenzo Peruggia linked to the painting?

Top of the Pucks

As of 2020, which seven ice hockey teams had won five or more Stanley Cups since the National Hockey League era began in 1918?

Mixed-up Countries

Below are anagrams of the names of twenty nation states from around the world. Can you unpick them to discover the countries?

A. mango oil

B. regalia

C. torn genome

D. a comedian

E. aneurism

F. serial

G. grey man

H. laced in

I. salad lover

J. also

K. prison age

L. enemy

M. acrimonies

N. moan

O. our hands

P. voice editor

Q. penal

R. lizard newts

S. moon race

T. lab user

Answers on pages 169–70

Rugby World Cup-Winning Captains

The inaugural rugby union world cup was held in 1987 and has been contested every four years since. Can you list the victorious captain who lifted the William Webb Ellis Trophy on each occasion?

A. 1987

B. 1991

C. 1995

D. 1999

E. 2003

F. 2007

G. 2011

H. 2015

I. 2019

A Capital Idea

Can you name South Africa's three capital cities (administrative, legislative and judicial)?

Answers on page 170

Picture This!

Which famous historical event is depicted here?
And what was the name of the poet who immortalized it in verse?

Hungry for Knowledge

What are the titles of the four books that make up Suzanne
Collins' Hunger Games series (the original trilogy and a prequel),
which inspired a series of Hollywood films?

Answers on page 170

The States of the Nation

Are you able to correctly label all fifty US states?

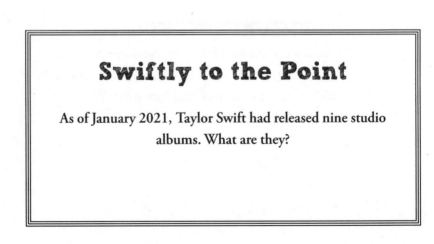

Swiftly to the Point

As of January 2021, Taylor Swift had released nine studio albums. What are they?

Noises Off

Can you recall which star-name performers provided the voices of these animated characters?

A. Branch from *Trolls*

B. Coraline Jones in *Coraline*

C. The Genie in *Aladdin*

D. Meg Griffin in *Family Guy*

E. Simba in *The Lion King*

F. Lucious Best in *The Incredibles*

G. Homer Simpson in *The Simpsons*

H. Dory in *Finding Nemo*

I. Stuart Little in *Stuart Little*

J. Eudora in *The Princess and the Frog*

K. Princess Mindy in *The Spongebob Squarepants Movie*

L. Unicron in *Transformers: The Movie*

M. Fiona in *Shrek*

N. Sullivan in *Monsters, Inc.*

O. Tigress in *Kung-Fu Panda*

Gulliver's Travels

Jonathan Swift's *Gulliver's Travels* is divided into four sections, each covering a specific voyage. What are the eight place names mentioned in the titles of those four sections?

Answers on page 172

Pasta Varieties

How good is your knowledge of Italian cuisine?
Identify the various types of pasta illustrated below.

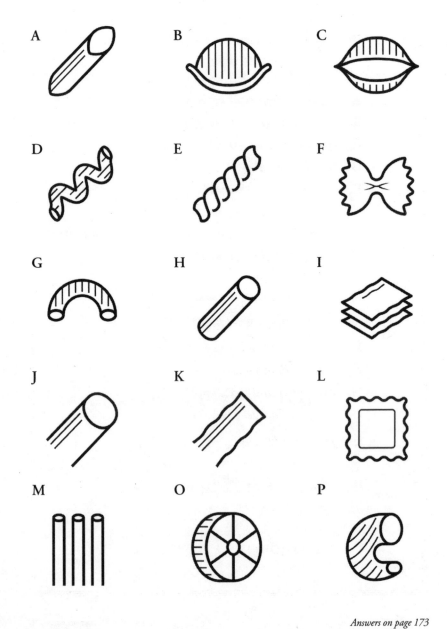

A

B

C

D

E

F

G

H

I

J

K

L

M

O

P

Answers on page 173

On the Record

Can you name the artists behind the following iconic rock albums?

A. *Bringing It All Back Home* (1965)

B. *Surrealistic Pillow* (1967)

C. *Disraeli Gears* (1967)

D. *Green River* (1969)

E. *Wish You Were Here?* (1975)

F. *Toys in the Attic* (1975)

G. *Darkness on the Edge of Town* (1978)

H. *Rust Never Sleeps* (1979)

I. *Eliminator* (1983)

J. *The Works* (1984)

K. *Slippery When Wet* (1986)

L. *Hysteria* (1987)

M. *Achtung Baby* (1991)

N. *The Colour and the Shape* (1997)

O. *Songs for The Deaf* (2002)

P. *Elephant* (2003)

Q. *American Idiot* (2004)

R. *Only by the Night* (2008)

S. *El Camino* (2011)

T. *AM* (2013)

U. *Blackstar* (2016)

Answer on page 174

Best of Enemies

Can you help Sherlock Holmes navigate a path from 221b Baker
Street to the headquarters of his criminal nemesis, Professor Moriarty?

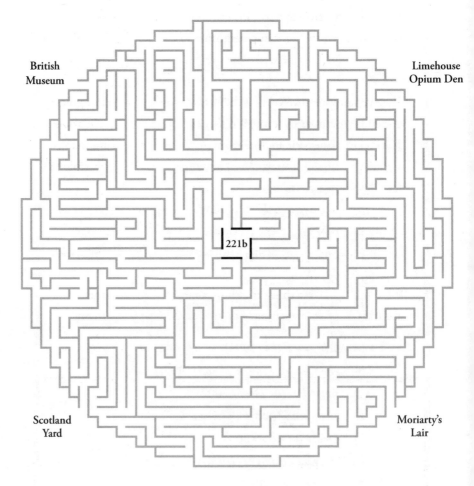

British
Museum

Limehouse
Opium Den

221b

Scotland
Yard

Moriarty's
Lair

Famous Last Words Part I

Below are the final lines from eight notable literary works.
Can you identify the novel and its author in each case?

A. 'So we beat on, boats against the current, borne back ceaselessly into the past.'

B. 'After all, tomorrow is another day.'

C. 'He turned out the light and went into Jem's room. He would be there all night, and he would be there when Jem waked up in the morning.'

D. 'The eyes and faces all turned themselves towards me, and guiding myself by them, as by a magical thread, I stepped into the room.'

E. 'The creatures outside looked from pig to man, and from man to pig, and from pig to man again; but already it was impossible to say which was which.'

F. 'Very few castaways can claim to have survived so long at sea as Mr. Patel, and none in the company of an adult Bengal tiger.'

G. 'It's funny. Don't ever tell anybody anything. If you do, you start missing everybody.'

H. 'It is a far, far better thing that I do, than I have ever done; it is a far, far better rest that I go to than I have ever known.'

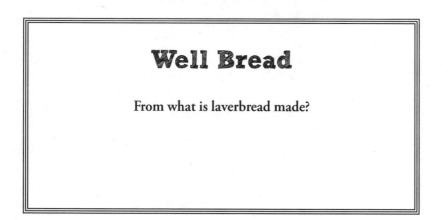

Well Bread

From what is laverbread made?

Answers on page 175

Dinosaurs Part I

Can you correctly identify the species of dinosaur from the drawings below?

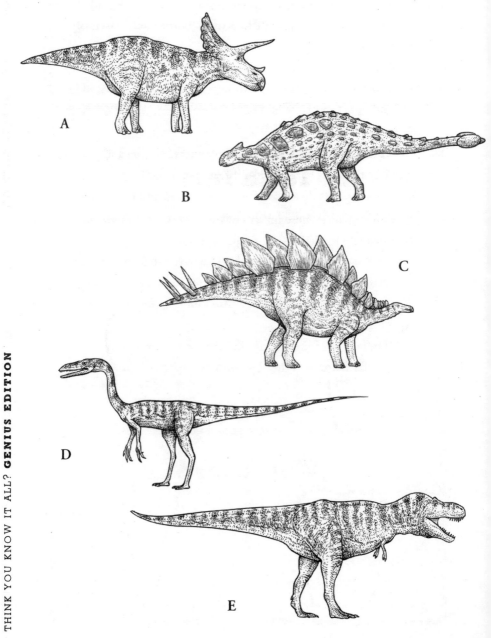

A

B

C

D

E

The Sum Total

What number do you get if you take John Buchan's Steps
and multiply it by the number of times a biscuit should
literally be baked?

Something to Get Your Teeth Into

Can you label these images of the four human teeth,
correctly identifying the type of tooth in each case?

A. B.

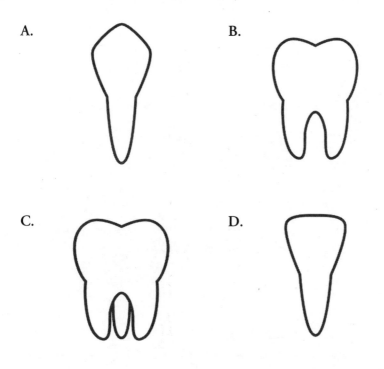

C. D.

Answers on page 175

Where the Heart Is

From which nations do these ten assorted international superstars originally hail?

A. Gotye

B. Björk

C. Gilberto Gil

D. Shakira

E. Keith Urban

F. Celia Cruz

G. Rihanna

H. Wyclef Jean

I. Youssou N'Dour

J. Carlos Santana

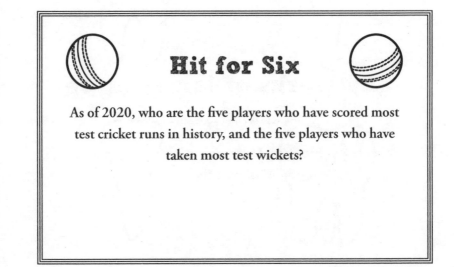

Hit for Six

As of 2020, who are the five players who have scored most test cricket runs in history, and the five players who have taken most test wickets?

World Cup Hosts

Can you name the cities that have hosted the final match
of each soccer World Cup since 1930?

A. 1930

B. 1934

C. 1938

D. 1950

E. 1954

F. 1958

G. 1962

H. 1966

I. 1970

J. 1974

K. 1978

L. 1982

M. 1986

N. 1990

O. 1994

P. 1998

Q. 2002

R. 2006

S. 2010

T. 2014

U. 2018

The Works of James Joyce

James Joyce published four prose works in his lifetime.
What were they?

Answers on page 176

Constellations

Can you correctly name the fourteen constellations illustrated below?

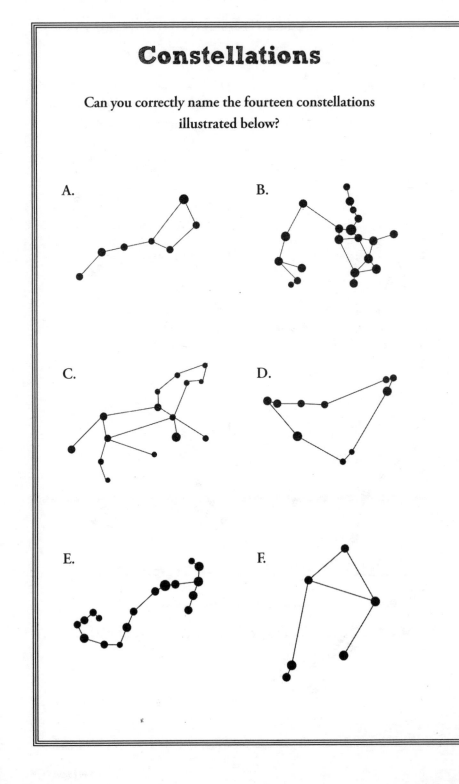

A.

B.

C.

D.

E.

F.

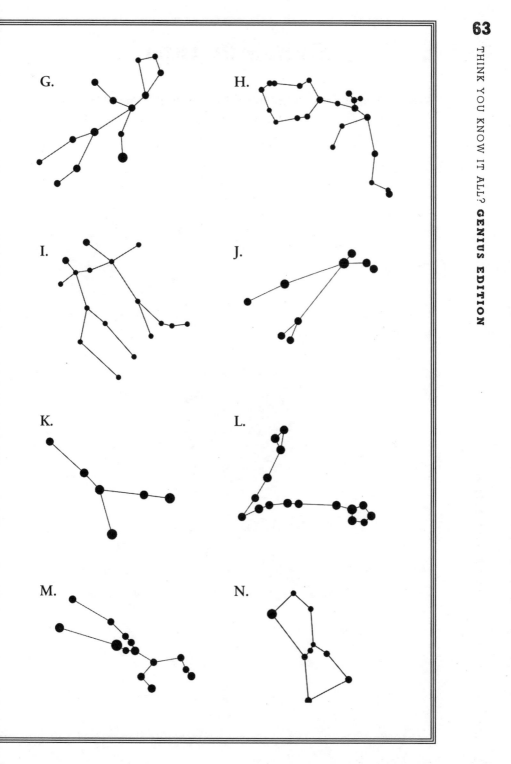

G.

H.

I.

J.

K.

L.

M.

N.

A Prime Example

A prime number is any number divisible only by one and itself.
The first ten prime numbers are 2, 3, 5, 7, 11, 13, 17, 19, 23
and 29. Can you list the next 20?

Slam Dunk

As of 2020, which ten sides have been champions of the National
Basketball Association (NBA) twice or more?

Answers on page 179

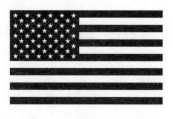

The Top Job

Nine US Vice-Presidents have taken over as President following either the death or resignation of the incumbent. Who are they?

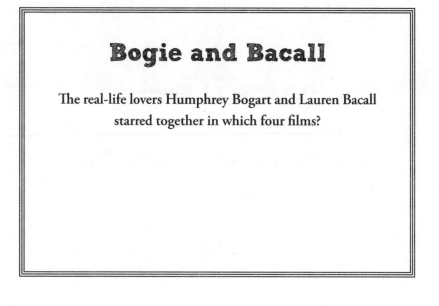

Bogie and Bacall

The real-life lovers Humphrey Bogart and Lauren Bacall starred together in which four films?

Answers on page 179

Spot the Difference

Can you spot five differences between these images of
Queen Elizabeth I?

The Works of Donna Tartt

As of 2020, the American writer Donna Tartt had written three
novels, each an international bestseller. What are they called?

When the Cape is Off

Below are eight famed superheroes but do you know by what names they are known in their everyday lives?

A. Captain America
B. Catwoman
C. Iceman
D. The Green Hornet
E. The Hulk
F. Iron Man
G. Magneto
H. Mr Fantastic
I. Robin
J. Supergirl
K. The Thing
L. Wonder Woman

The Antagonists of Rocky

Can you name the opponents faced by Rocky Balboa (or, in the case of Creed and Creed II, Rocky's protege Adonis Creed) in the climatic fight of each movie in the celebrated cinematic series?

A. Rocky

B. Rocky II

C. Rocky III

D. Rocky IV

E. Rocky V

F. Rocky Balboa

G. Creed

H. Creed II

Answers on page 181

De Niro and Pacino

In which four movies have Robert De Niro and Al Pacino appeared together?

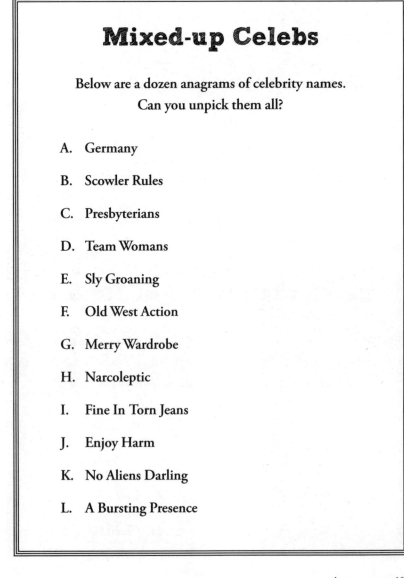

Mixed-up Celebs

Below are a dozen anagrams of celebrity names.
Can you unpick them all?

A. Germany

B. Scowler Rules

C. Presbyterians

D. Team Womans

E. Sly Groaning

F. Old West Action

G. Merry Wardrobe

H. Narcoleptic

I. Fine In Torn Jeans

J. Enjoy Harm

K. No Aliens Darling

L. A Bursting Presence

Answers on page 181

Name that Artist Part I

Can you name the artists who created each of these masterpieces?

A.

B.

C.

D.

Answers on page 182

Musical Maths

What number do you get if you take the original number of members of the Bee Gees and multiply them by the number of ways there are to leave your lover (according to Paul Simon), then subtract the number in the name of the band that had a hit with 'Love Shack'?

Hard Cheese

Which enzyme is added to milk in the manufacture of most hard cheeses?

Answers on page 182

All in the Mind

Can you correctly label this diagram of the human brain?

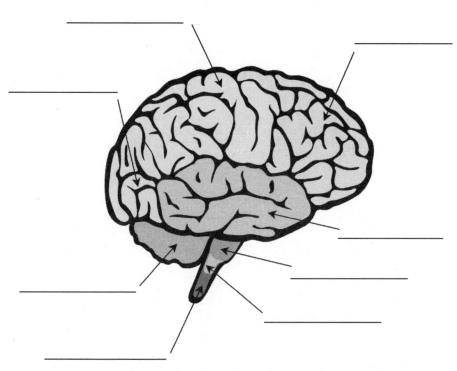

The Helpless Shah

Which game is often ended by a phrase that derives from the Persian for 'The Shah is Helpless'?

Answers on pages 182–3

Gilbert and Sullivan

From which of the roster of G&S operettas do the following songs come?

A. 'A British Tar'

B. 'Nightmare Song'

C. 'My eyes are fully open'

D. 'When I, good friends, was called to the bar'

E. 'I've got a little list'

F. 'My name is John Wellington-Wells'

G. 'So go to him and say to him'

H. 'The Major-General's Song'

I. 'If you give me your attention'

J. 'Take a pair of sparkling eyes'

K. 'I have a song to sing, O!'

Little but Perfectly Formed

Which five dwarf planets are recognized by the International Astronomical Union?

Dingbats Part II

Can you decipher the famous names from the visual clues below?

A.

B.

C.

Don Quixote

What is the name of Don Quixote's companion in
Miguel de Cervantes's celebrated novel?

Answer on page 183

Who's on First Base?

Below is a visual representation of the standard positions on a baseball pitch. Can you fill in each label with the appropriate position?

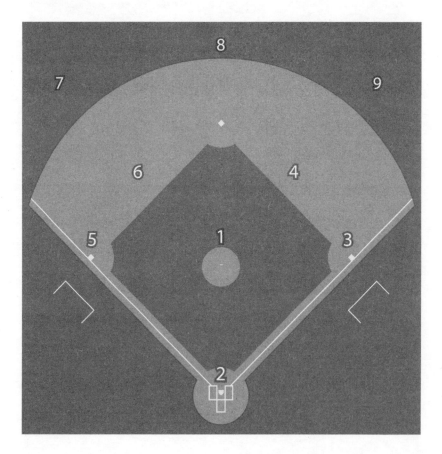

Africa's Capitals

Can you name the capital city of the following African nations?

A. Angola

B. Benin

C. Burkina Faso

D. Democratic Republic of the Congo

E. Republic of the Congo

F. Eritrea

G. Gabon

H. Lesotho

I. Liberia

J. Malawi

K. Morocco

L. Namibia

M. Nigeria

N. Rwanda

O. Senegal

P. Somalia

Q. Tanzania

R. Togo

S. Uganda

T. Zambia

Hard to Categorize

Can you name the eight major standard taxonomic rankings
used in biological classification?

Answers on page 184

Literary Lovers

Here are some of the most fabled romantic couplings in literary history but in which book does each couple appear and who were their creators?

A. Ennis Del Mar and Jack Twist

B. Florentino Ariza and Fermina Daza

C. Henry DeTamble and Clare Anne Abshire

D. Catherine Earnshaw and Heathcliff

E. Hazel Grace Lancaster and Augustus Waters

F. Katniss Everdeen and Peeta Mellark

G. Oliver Barrett IV and Jennifer Cavilleri

H. Constance Reid and Oliver Mellors

I. Jake Barnes and Lady Brett Ashley

Sporting Terms

In which sport might you perform a Rudolph and a Randolph?

Answers on page 184

An Odyssey Through Homer

Homer's *Odyssey* is considered among the greatest products of classical civilization but how much do you know about it? Odysseus is the main protagonist but can you name the characters from the descriptions below?

A. Odysseus's wife

B. Their princely son

C. A loyal shepherd

D. A beautiful nymph whose home is Ogygia

E. A witch-goddess who turns Odysseus's crew into swine

F. A goddess who frequently appears in disguise as Mentor, a friend of Odysseus

G. Odysseus's aging father

H. The King of Pylos

I. The King of Sparta

J. His wife, the Queen

Answers on page 185

The League of Extraordinary Gentlemen

In the 2003 movie *The League of Extraordinary Gentlemen* (based on the popular comic book series), can you remember which characters with rich literary pasts were played by each of the following actors?

A. Sean Connery

B. Naseeruddin Shah

C. Peta Wilson

D. Stuart Townsend

E. Shane West

F. Jason Flemyng

G. Terry O'Neill

Sounds About Right

The human inner ear contains three tiny bones.
Do you know what they are called?

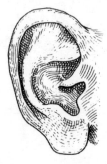

Royal Love

Below is a list of famous lovers of European rulers over the centuries. But can you connect each name to the monarch with whom they were romantically involved?

A. Grigory Potemkin

B. Virginia de Castiglione

C. Nell Gwyn

D. Madame de Pompadour

E. Maria Fitzherbert

F. Freda Dudley Ward

G. Marie Walewska

H. Louise de La Vallière

I. Lillie Langtry

J. Anna Mons

Amazing Amazon

The River Amazon runs through which three countries?

Answers on page 185

Indian Cuisine

Do you know the Indian terms for the following types of food?

A. Potato
B. Lentils
C. Cauliflower
D. Chicken
E. Spinach
F. Iced yoghurt drink
G. Meat, typically lamb or mutton

Shakespearean Characters

In which Shakespeare plays do each of these characters appear?

A. Benedick
B. Miranda
C. Friar Laurence
D. Portia
E. Orlando
F. Katharina
G. Brabantio
H. Cassandra
I. Iras
J. Fenton
K. Mistress Overdone
L. Sir Toby Belch

Three Sides to Every Story

Can you correctly classify the six types of triangle shown below?

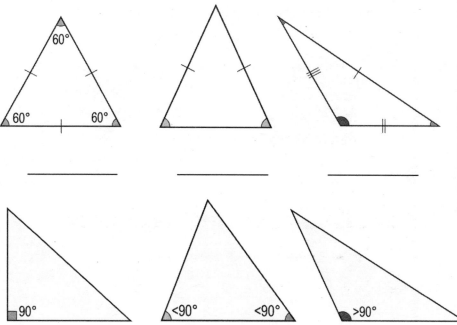

Home Run!

As of 2020, who are the ten players with the highest all-time number of home runs in Major League Baseball?

Answer on pages 186–7

In Bloom

How green-fingered are you? Below are images of an array of common flowers but how many can you correctly identify?

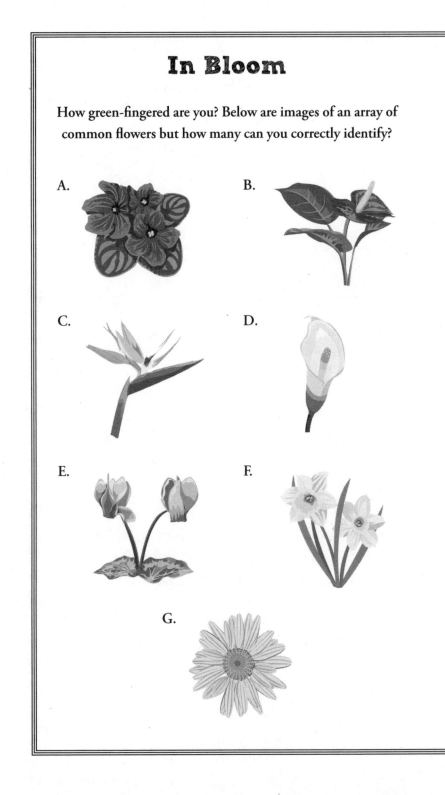

A.

B.

C.

D.

E.

F.

G.

H.

I.

J.

K.

L.

M.

N.

O.

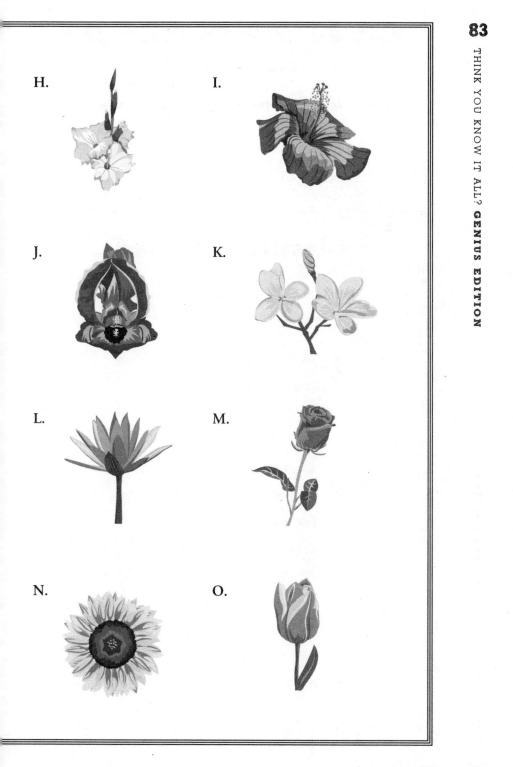

Prix de L'Arc de Triomphe

On which Paris racecourse is the Prix de l'Arc de Triomphe run?

Classical Classics

Below are listed some of the greatest literary masterpieces from antiquity. But to which authors are they traditionally credited?

A.   *The Twelve Caesars*

B.   *Medea*

C.   *The Art of War*

D.   *Meno*

E.   *The Metamorphoses*

F.   *Antigone*

G.   *Lysistrata*

H.   *The Satyricon*

I.   *The Iliad*

J.   *The Aeneid*

K.   *Prometheus Bound*

L.   *Bhagavad Gita*

M.   *Germania*

Yoga Positions

It's one thing to be able to bend your body in incredible ways, but how mindful are you of the names of these classic yoga poses?

A.

B.

C.

D.

E.

F.

G.

H.

Answers on page 188

Who's on Drums?

Can you name the classic line-ups of the bands below?

Guns N' Roses

The Who

Fleetwood Mac

REM

The Police

Nirvana

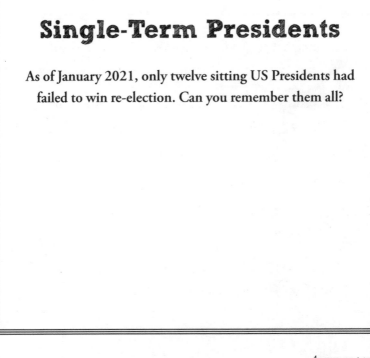

Single-Term Presidents

As of January 2021, only twelve sitting US Presidents had failed to win re-election. Can you remember them all?

Answers on page 189

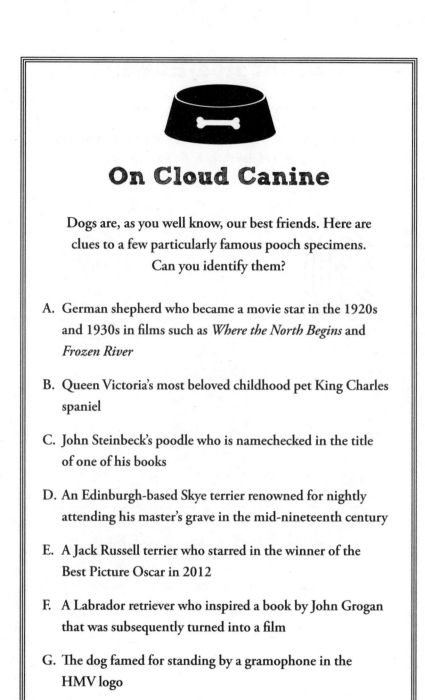

On Cloud Canine

Dogs are, as you well know, our best friends. Here are
clues to a few particularly famous pooch specimens.
Can you identify them?

A. German shepherd who became a movie star in the 1920s
and 1930s in films such as *Where the North Begins* and
Frozen River

B. Queen Victoria's most beloved childhood pet King Charles
spaniel

C. John Steinbeck's poodle who is namechecked in the title
of one of his books

D. An Edinburgh-based Skye terrier renowned for nightly
attending his master's grave in the mid-nineteenth century

E. A Jack Russell terrier who starred in the winner of the
Best Picture Oscar in 2012

F. A Labrador retriever who inspired a book by John Grogan
that was subsequently turned into a film

G. The dog famed for standing by a gramophone in the
HMV logo

H. The dog that found the Jules Rimet trophy (the football
World Cup) after it was stolen in 1966

Answers on page 190

Caught Red-Handed

Fingerprints were introduced into the world of crime detection in the nineteenth century since each person's fingerprints are unique. Do you know the names of the three basic patters used in fingerprint analysis, illustrated below?

A.

B.

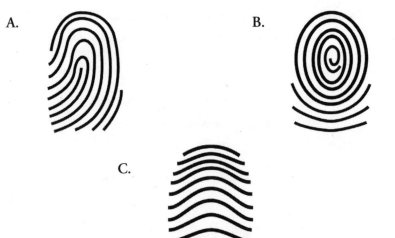

C.

Elementary, My Dear Quizzer

A number of chemical elements are named after people. Here is a list of abbreviations for some of those elements. Can you work out what the element is and after whom it was named?

Abbreviation	Element name	Person
Gd		
Cm		
Bk		
Es		
Fm		
Md		
No		
Lr		
Rf		
Bh		
Mt		
Rg		
Cn		
Lv		
Og		

Answers on page 191

What the Dickens?

Dickens populated his literary world with some of the most memorable characters in the English language. In which of his stories do the following characters appear?

A. Inspector Bucket

B. Dick Datchery

C. John Harmon

D. Arthur Clennam

E. Mrs Hominy

F. Mr Jaggers

G. Alfred Jingle

H. Will Fern

I. Lucie Manette

J. Mr Sowerberry

K. Professor Wigsby

L. Jacob Marley

M. Thomas Gradgrind

N. Newman Noggs

O. Dora Spenlow

Kafka-esque

What are the names of Franz Kafka's three full-length novels?

Answers on page 192

Is it a Bird, is it a Plane?

Here is a selection of screen interpretations of perhaps the ultimate superhero, Superman. But do you know who played the lead in each?

A. *Superman & The Mole Men* (1951)

B. *Superman IV: The Quest for Peace* (1987)

C. *Superboy* (1988)

D. *The Adventures of Superboy* (1989–1991)

E. *Lois & Clark: The New Adventures of Superman* (1993–1997)

F. *Smallville* (2001–2011)

G. *Superman Returns* (2006)

H. *Man of Steel* (2013)

In Tune

Below are illustrated some standard musical notes.
Can you correctly name each and give its relative note value?

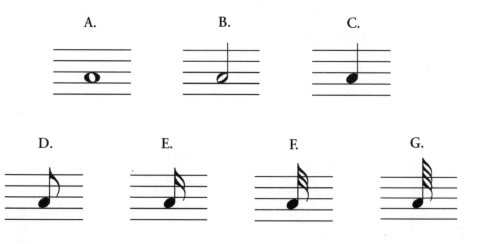

Answers on page 192

The Characters of Frozen

How much do you know about the Disney classic, *Frozen*?
Can you identify the characters from the descriptions below?

A. The young queen of Arendelle

B. The queen's younger sister

C. Their snowman companion

D. The Sámi iceman

E. The iceman's reindeer

F. Prince of the Southern Isles

G. The proprietor of a trading post and sauna

H. The wise troll who rules the Valley of the Living Rock

I. An enchanted snow monster who protects the queen's palace

Assassins

Who were the infamous assassins of the following eminent
public figures?

A. Archduke Franz Ferdinand

B. Martin Luther King, Jr.

C. Spencer Perceval

D. John F. Kennedy

E. William McKinley

F. Anna Lindh

G. Mahatma Gandhi

H. Rajiv Gandhi

Answers on pages 192–3

Musical Rivals

As depicted in the 1984 Oscar-winning film *Amadeus*, who was
Mozart's composer nemesis?

Flower Power

What do you remember of your school biology lessons?
How accurately can you label the diagram of a flower below?

Answers on page 193

Champion of Champions

The European Cup for club soccer was first contested in 1955 (and rebranded as the UEFA Champions League in 1992). Between 1955 and 2020, twelve club sides had won the competition at least twice. But which sides?

Cracking the Latin Code

Below is an important coded message. To read it, you must test your knowledge of Roman numerals. Each letter is represented by a number in a simple substitution code: A = 1, B = 2, C = 3 and so on to Z = 26. Each letter in the code is represented by a one- or two-digit number as indicated by the number of dashes.

_/_/_/_/_/__ _/__ _/_/_/_

Solve the following sums, converting the Roman numerals into ordinary numbers. When you have your answer to each sum, insert the digits in order into the code. Each digit corresponds to a dash. Then convert the numbers into letters and, hey presto, the message will emerge!

Sums

V – II = ?

III x V = ?

(XII x XVI) – 1 = ?

II x IX = ?

(IX x CII) + 1 = ?

(IV x X) + V = ?

VII x II = ?

Answers on page 194

Miss Marple

Agatha Christie wrote twelve novels featuring her detective, Miss Marple. Can you remember them all?

I Like Your Style

Can you identify the four artistic styles on display in these pictures?

A.

B.

C.

D.

Answers on page 194

A Whole Lot of History

Below are a selection of pivotal events in human history from across the millennia. Are you up to the challenge of giving the correct year when each event took place?

A. The foundation of Rome

B. Egypt is conquered by Alexander the Great

C. Roman Emperor Constantine converts to Christianity

D. Charlemagne is crowned Holy Roman Emperor

E. The Magna Carta is signed by England's King John

F. Fall of Constantinople to the Ottoman Turks

G. Christopher Columbus sails to the New World

H. William Shakespeare is born

I. Isaac Newton publishes *Principia Mathematica*

J. The French Revolution begins

K. Charles Darwin publishes *The Origin of Species*

L. New Zealand becomes the world's first country to introduce unrestricted women's suffrage

M. Albert Einstein publishes his Theory of Special Relativity

N. The October Revolution sweeps Lenin to power in Russia

O. Communist China is founded

P. The collapse of the Berlin Wall

Q. Nelson Mandela becomes President of South Africa

Answers on pages 194–5

Stans of the World

There are seven nations that end with the suffix '-stan'.
Can you name them all?

Disney Anthems

Can you remember from which classic Disney films these
anthems come?

A. 'Shiny'

B. 'Trust in Me'

C. 'Part of Your World'

D. 'Into the Unknown'

E. 'Baby Mine'

F. 'Feed the Birds'

G. 'When You Wish Upon a Star'

H. 'Remember Me'

I. 'A Whole New World'

J. 'Siamese Cat Song'

K. 'Be Prepared'

L. 'Be Our Guest'

M. 'When Will My Life Begin'

N. 'A Dream Is a Wish Your Heart Makes'

O. 'You've Got a Friend in Me'

Answers on page 195

A Rock and a Hard Place

There are three main classifications of rocks, which are derived
from the physical changes a rock undergoes as a result of,
for instance, melting, cooling, eroding, compacting or
deforming. But can you recall what these classifications are?

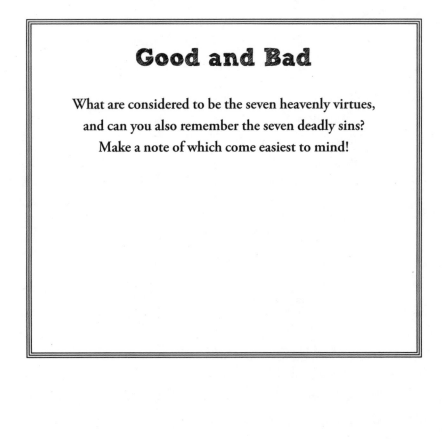

Good and Bad

What are considered to be the seven heavenly virtues,
and can you also remember the seven deadly sins?
Make a note of which come easiest to mind!

The Deities of Ancient Egypt

The ancient Egyptians had a vast pantheon of gods and goddesses,
some more benevolent than others. Below are images of just
a handful of the most prominent. Which of them can you
correctly name?

A.

B.

C.

D.

E.

F.

G.

H.

Answers on page 196

Trivial Pursuits

Can you recall the six categories of question in the classic
version of Trivial Pursuit, and their colours?

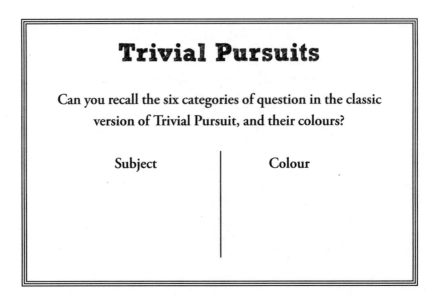

Subject | Colour

Head in the Clouds

Below are illustrated eight common cloud types.
How many can you accurately identify?

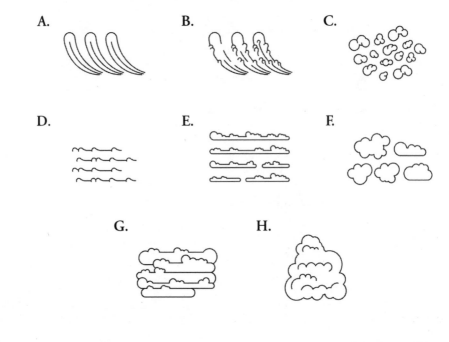

A.

B.

C.

D.

E.

F.

G.

H.

Buddhist Truths

What are the Four Noble Truths of Buddhism?

Poems (Not) by Wordsworth

Which of the following poems is not by William Wordsworth?

'Daffodils'

'Tintern Abbey'

'Ode to a Nightingale'

'Ode: Intimations of Immortality'

'The Solitary Reaper'

'London 1802'

Answers on page 197

Highs and Lows

In the Western classical choral tradition, what are the
seven traditional vocal-type classifications?

The Lives of the Wives

Henry VIII is perhaps most famous for the number of wives he
had – six in total. Can you name them all in the right order,
describe how the marriage ended in each case, and list any
named children that they had together?

Name	Fate of Marriage	Children

Dinosaurs Part II

Can you correctly identify the species of dinosaur from their skeletons below?

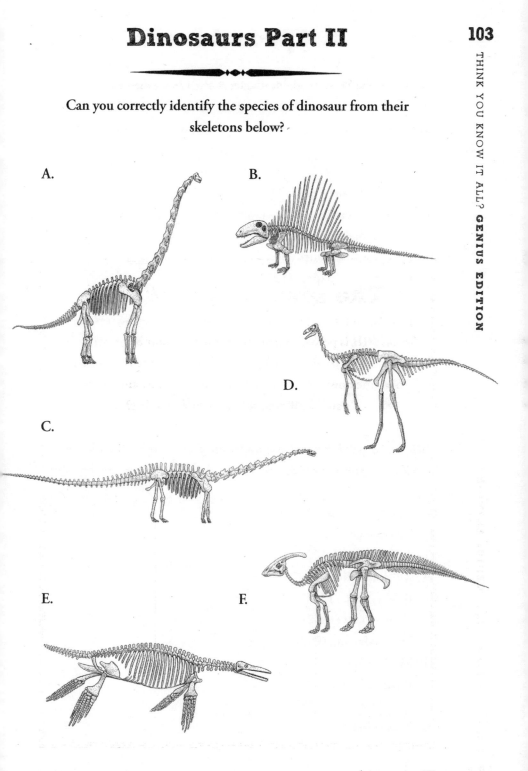

A.

B.

D.

C.

E.

F.

Answers on page 198

Space Race

Below are listed a few highlights from the US–Soviet space race that came to pass in the decades after the Second World War. Can you name the missions that achieved each milestone, and the individuals involved?

A. First dog in orbit (1957)
B. First Humanoid animal (a chimpanzee) in space (1961)
C. First human spaceflight (1961)
D. First pilot-controlled space flight (1961)
E. First woman in space (1963)
F. First spacewalk (1965)
G. First man on the moon (1969; for bonus points, who was the second man and who remained in the command module?)

Eurovision Champs

Below is a list of victors from down the years in the Eurovision Song Contest. But for which countries did they bring the title home?

A. Jean-Claude Pascal (1961)
B. Séverine (1971)
C. Teach-In (1975)
D. Milk and Honey (1979)
E. Bobbysocks! (1985)
F. Celine Dion (1988)
G. Linda Martin (1992)
H. Marie N (2002)
I. Ruslana (2004)
J. Conchita Wurst (2014)
K. Netta (2018)

Answers on pages 198–9

If the Shoe Fits

Can you name the styles of the classic men's shoes illustrated below?

A.

B.

C.

D.

E.

F.

The Pillars of Islam

What are the Five Pillars of Islam?

Answers on page 199

Name that Artist Part II

Can you name the artists who created each of these masterpieces?

A.

B.

C.

D.

E.

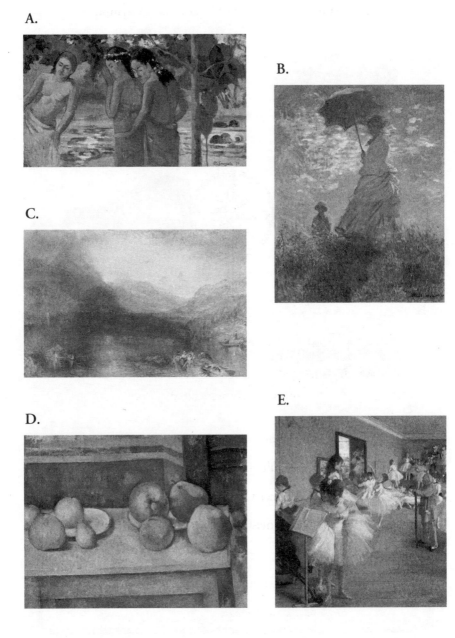

Answers on page 199

Sporting Figures

What do you get if you add the number of players in a basketball team to the number of Usain Bolt's Olympic titles?

Aye, Aye Cap'n!

With which vessels are the following sailors of fact and fiction most closely associated?

A. Jason

B. William Bligh

C. James Cook

D. Francis Drake

E. Captain Ahab

F. Blackbeard

G. Lord Nelson

Answers on page 200

Layers of the Earth

Can you accurately identify the five layers of the Earth, illustrated below?

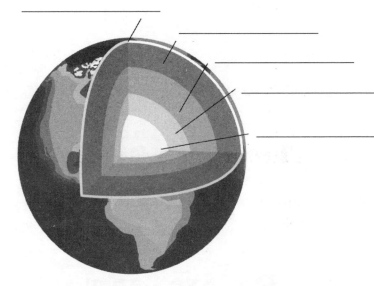

Better than the Original?

The following books are all sequels but can you identify the original novels that they follow on from?

A. *Closing Time*
B. *The Starlight Barking*
C. *Little Men*
D. *Porno*
E. *Go Set a Watchman*
F. *The Mysterious Island*
G. *The Sicilian*
H. *Twenty Years After*

Answers on pages 200–1

The Country Formerly Known As ...

Which country changed its name to Eswatini in 2018?

Throwing a Googly

Below is a visual representation of the standard fielding positions on a cricket pitch. Can you fill in each label with the appropriate position?

1. _____

2. _____

3. _____

4. _____

5. _____

6. _____

7. _____

8. _____

9. _____

10. _____

Answers on page 201

The Movies of John Grisham

Can you name the seven feature films made for cinematic release
that were based on legal thrillers by John Grisham?

Poker Face

Can you name all ten poker hands?

Answers on page 201

Super Bowl

As of 2021, who are the only two NFL competitors to have won five or more Super Bowl rings as players? And who has the most rings of all (eight) gained as player (two) and coach (six)?

Ocean's 11

Who were the actors who played the members of the eponymous eleven in the 2001 (*Ocean's Eleven*) remake of the classic heist movie (*Ocean's 11*) originally released in 1960? Below are their character names to give you a helping hand.

A. Danny Ocean

B. Frank Catton

C. Robert 'Rusty' Ryan

D. Reuben Tishkoff

E. Virgil Malloy

F. Turk Malloy

G. Livingston Dell

H. Basher Tarr

I. 'The Amazing' Yen

J. Saul Bloom

K. Linus Caldwell

Answers on page 202

What Goes Around Comes Around

In Dante Alighieri's fourteenth-century poetical masterpiece, *The Divine Comedy*, can you remember each of the nine concentric circles of hell that he describes in *Inferno*?

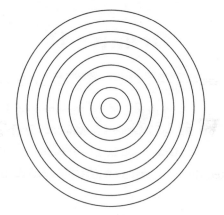

Group Think

By what group nouns are the following types of animal known?

A. Cheetahs

B. Cockroaches

C. Owls

D. Apes

E. Rhinoceros

F. Porcupines

G. Dolphins

H. Hippopotamuses

Answers on page 202

A Herculean Challenge

According to classical mythology, what were the twelve labours of Hercules?

What Do You See?

Who painted the image below and what specific location does it depict?

Political Number-Crunching

What do you get if you add the number of EU member states to the number of colonies that formed the United States?

A Place Called Home

From which countries do (or did) the following celebrated authors originally come from?

A. Paulo Coelho

B. Margaret Atwood

C. Gabriel Garcia Marquez

D. Haruki Murakami

E. Olga Tokarczuk

F. Umberto Eco

G. Tan Twan Eng

H. Arundhati Roy

I. J. M. Coetzee

J. Markus Zusak

K. Carlos Ruiz Zafón

L. Ben Okri

Answers on page 203

Three Wise Men

According to Western Christian tradition (though not stated in the Bible), what were the names of the three magi kings and where did they rule?

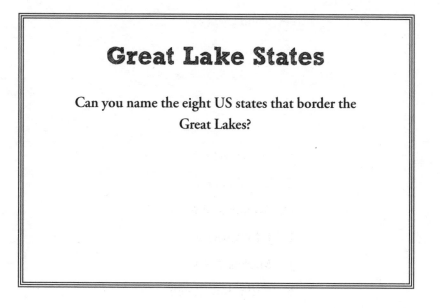

Great Lake States

Can you name the eight US states that border the Great Lakes?

Answers on page 203

Join the Dots

Join the dots – whose is the famous face?

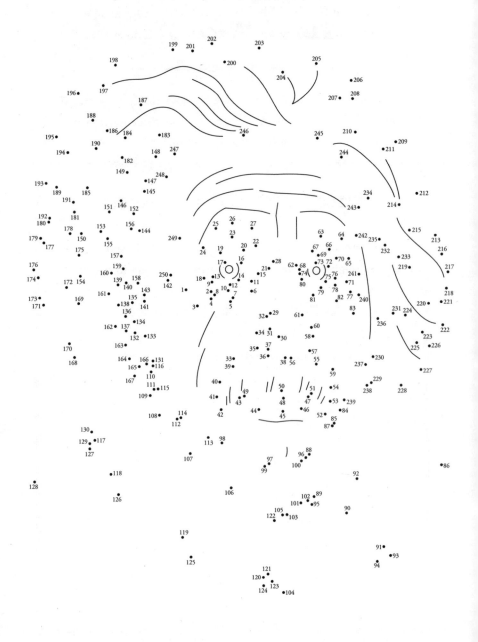

Answers on page 204

The Novels of
George R. R. Martin

What are the titles of the five published novels plus the two projected final volumes in George R. R. Martin's A Song of Ice and Fire cycle, upon which the television series *Game of Thrones* was based?

Sports of Champions

Below are a list of some of the greatest names in sport from through the years but in which disciplines did they each flourish?

A. Jahangir Khan

B. Alberto Tomba

C. Brian Boitano

D. Lin Dan

E. Andy Fordham

F. Jan Frodeno

G. Eric Heiden

H. Pieter van den Hoogenband

I. David Bryant

Answer on page 205

Rub-a-dub-dub

According to the nursery rhyme, who were the three men in a tub?

Best Actors Never to Have Won an Oscar

The Oscars offer the ultimate acting accolade and here are some of the big stars who can boast of winning one of the little statuettes. However, there are two actors among them who, as of 2021, were still yet to receive the award. Can you spot them?

Casey Affleck

Jennifer Lawrence

Tom Cruise

Hillary Swank

Sean Penn

Sandra Bullock

Jack Nicholson

Glenn Close

Nicholas Cage

Reese Witherspoon

William Hurt

Jessica Lange

Answers on page 205

Classical Architecture

Here are five columns each reflecting one of the five orders of classical architecture. But can you correctly name each order?

A.

B.

C.

D.

E.

Answers on page 205

Motown

Founded by Berry Gordy Jr as Tamla Records in 1959, the Motown record label has spread soulful joy around the world for decades. Here are just a few of the great records it has released, but can you say which artists first made these songs famous?

A. 'Ain't No Mountain High Enough'

B. 'Papa was a Rollin' Stone"

C. 'What Becomes of the Brokenhearted'

D. 'Sir Duke'

E. 'My Guy'

F. 'Heaven Must Have Sent You'

G. 'Reflections'

H. 'End of The Road'

I. 'Does Your Mama Know About Me'

J. 'Please Mr Postman'

The Pentateuch

Which five books make up the Pentateuch in the Jewish faith?

Answers on pages 205–6

The World of Wine

Here are some leading wine brands from around the world
but do you know from which countries they originate?

A. Concha Y Toro

B. Gallo

C. Changyu

D. Yellow Tail

E. J. Hofstätter

F. Oyster Bay

G. Vega Sicilia

H. Sharphams

I. Esporáo

J. Heimann

K. Leitz

L. Fanagoria

M. Millstream

N. Chateau Mukhrani Saperavi

Words and Numbers

What do you get if you multiply the number of novels in the Harry
Potter series by the number of Joseph Heller's 'Catch'?

Answers on page 206

Turning Over a New Leaf

How good are you on your arboriculture?
Can you identify the tree species from their leaves?

A.

B.

C.

D.

E.

F.

G.

Answers on page 206

Famous Last Words Part II

Below are the final lines of another eight notable literary works.
Can you identify the novel and its author in each case?

A. 'Up out of the lampshade, startled by the overhead light,
flew a large nocturnal butterfly that began circling the room.
The strains of the piano and violin rose up weakly from below.'

B. 'But that is the beginning of a new story – the story of the gradual
renewal of a man, the story of his gradual regeneration, of his
passing from one world into another, of his initiation into a new
unknown life. That might be the subject of a new story, but our
present story is ended.'

C. 'A LAST NOTE FROM YOUR NARRATOR. I am haunted by
humans.'

D. 'Are there any questions?'

E. 'For all to be accomplished, for me to feel less lonely, all that
remained to hope was that on the day of my execution there
should be a huge crowd of spectators and that they should greet
me with howls of execration.'

F. 'I lingered round them, under that benign sky; watched the moths
fluttering among the heath, and hare-bells; listened to the soft
wind breathing through the grass; and wondered how anyone
could ever imagine unquiet slumbers, for the sleepers in that
quiet earth.'

G. 'I got to light out for the Territory ahead of the rest, because Aunt
Sally she's going to adopt me and sivilize me, and I can't stand it.
I been there before.'

H. 'Old father, old artificer, stand me now and ever in good stead.'

I. 'One bird said to Billy Pilgrim, "Poo-tee-weet?"'

Answers on page 207

The Avengers

Can you recall the original line-up of Marvel's *The Avengers*?

Say When

How good is your historical recall? In which years of the twentieth century did the following important events occur?

(Give yourself a pat on the back for getting within a year either side of the correct answers.)

A. The Wright Brothers make the first controlled heavier-than-air flight

B. The RMS *Titanic* sinks on its maiden voyage from Southampton to New York

C. Alexander Fleming discovers penicillin

D. Adolf Hitler becomes German Chancellor

E. India wins independence from British rule

F. Bill Haley and His Comets release 'Rock Around the Clock' to usher in the rock 'n' roll age

G. The assassination of Martin Luther King Jr.

H. Richard Nixon resigns as US President

I. MTV is launched

J. Google is founded by Larry Page and Sergey Brin

Answers on page 207

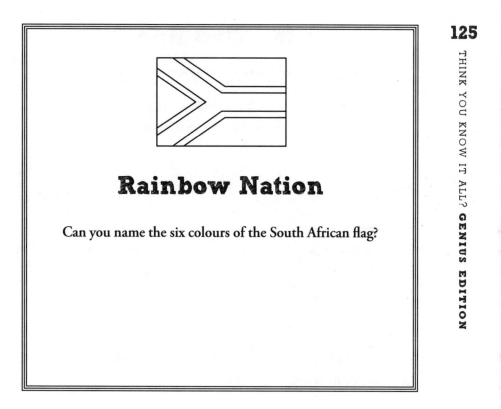

Rainbow Nation

Can you name the six colours of the South African flag?

The Modern Pentathlon

Which five events make up the modern pentathlon?

Answers on page 207

In the Dog House

How knowledgeable are you about our canine friends?
Can you identify the breeds of dog illustrated below?

A.

B.

C.

D.

E.

F.

G.

H.

I.

J.

K.

L.

Wimbledon Winners

Wimbledon is arguably the most prized of all the tennis Grand Slams and here is a roll call of some of its illustrious past winners. There are, however two names in the list who never lifted the winners' trophies. Do you know who?

Richard Krajicek

Lindsay Davenport

Pat Cash

Monica Seles

Conchita Martínez

Ken Rosewall

Angelique Kerber

Lleyton Hewitt

Amélie Mauresmo

Stan Smith

Jana Novotná

Jan Kodeš

Monopoly!

In the popular boardgame Monopoly, what are the squares at each corner of the board?

The Cities of Ireland

Can you name the five cities in the Republic of Ireland?

_____   _____

_____   _____

_____

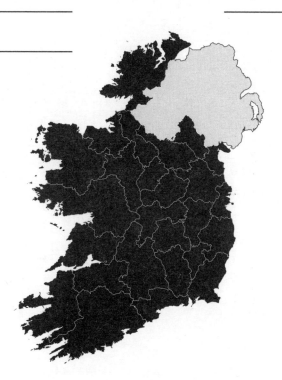

Feeling the Heat

What are the three types of heat transfer?

Answers on pages 210–11

General Knowledge Wordsearch

Now, the ultimate wordsearch. To determine what words you need to find, solve the general knowledge clues below. The words in the grid may be up, down, diagonal, forwards or backwards. Good luck!

L	T	K	N	S	N	X	W	O	E	D	K	V	X	R	Q	W	X	S	Z	R	C	Q
O	L	E	A	H	P	A	R	V	Y	E	N	K	C	O	H	D	I	V	A	D	M	H
A	N	Z	D	B	H	F	M	E	R	E	N	G	U	E	M	K	Z	A	Q	O	L	E
C	M	S	V	U	I	O	X	R	N	L	D	X	X	A	B	L	J	G	Z	M	F	C
A	Y	E	T	A	K	N	X	S	C	X	G	E	T	T	Y	S	B	U	R	G	N	S
S	K	R	G	A	C	E	I	F	C	K	C	F	C	L	G	D	B	N	M	I	L	Y
I	O	G	N	D	S	V	E	K	e	R	E	I	S	U	B	R	O	C	B	S	M	Z
N	Q	E	O	Z	I	H	V	L	O	U	B	M	T	G	Y	S	J	F	D	U	U	E
O	A	I	R	Z	K	T	G	G	L	L	U	E	L	C	F	J	N	M	V	L	P	V
R	P	B	Y	E	O	Y	C	A	Z	I	A	M	O	A	D	K	F	W	V	E	W	A
O	W	U	B	R	T	J	J	P	B	B	N	T	E	J	T	Z	O	C	C	I	Q	H
Y	D	B	D	Y	X	E	Q	R	N	A	K	G	E	X	G	N	V	T	I	M	Y	C
A	G	K	R	C	K	L	T	R	F	G	T	B	T	S	L	H	E	X	V	A	F	O
L	V	A	O	X	C	I	C	E	R	O	L	J	W	O	L	I	Z	M	J	N	C	G
E	K	K	L	I	T	L	Z	W	Q	H	I	U	M	S	N	A	X	U	M	V	N	U
M	C	D	O	G	R	U	B	S	R	E	T	E	P	T	S	F	R	E	S	E	G	H

A. Twice made James Bond movie (1967 and 2006)

B. Jazz legend whose signature tune was 'Take the "A" Train'

C. The capital of Russia for most of the period 1713–1918

D. Artist responsible for the 'School of Athens' fresco in the Vatican

E. Famous Swiss cheese that originated in the canton of Bern

F. The poet-father of computing pioneer, Ada Lovelace

G. First name of the celebrated leader of the Ottoman Empire from 1520 to 1566

H. Turkmenistan's capital city

I. A style of music and dance originating in the Dominican Republic

J. Artist whose works include *The Splash* and *Mr and Mrs Clark and Percy*

K. Ukrainian-born pole-vaulting legend who broke the world record thirty-five times

L. Site of legendary address by Abraham Lincoln delivered on 19 November 1863

M. Roman statesman and writer (106-43 BC) whose works include *De Re Publica (On the Commonwealth)* and *De Legibus (On the Laws)*

N. Visionary inventor, engineer and scientist born in the Austrian Empire who claimed to have been in love with a pigeon

O. Venezuela's leader from 1999–2013

P. Name by which Charles-Édouard Jeanneret-Gris, giant of twentieth-century architecture, is better known

Answers on page 211

British Prime Ministers

Can you name the ten longest-serving British Prime Ministers?

All Aboard the Ark

According to the Bible, what were the names of Noah's three sons?

Answers on page 212

The Earth's Atmosphere

The Earth's atmosphere is often divided into five main layers.
Can you label them on the image below?

The Five Stages of Grief

According to the famous Kübler-Ross model, what are the
five stages of grief?

Answers on page 213

In the words of POTUS Part II

It is a well-trodden path for those who ascend to the presidency
of the United States of America to tell their side of the story.
Here are the titles of six autobiographical works by former Presidents.

But which of them wrote which?

A. *An American Life*

B. *Mr. Citizen*

C. *In the Arena: A Memoir of Victory,
Defeat, and Renewal*

D. *A World Transformed*

E. *A Promised Land*

F. *The Rough Riders*

Rivers of Hades

What, in Greek mythology, are considered to be the five
rivers of Hades?

Answers on page 214

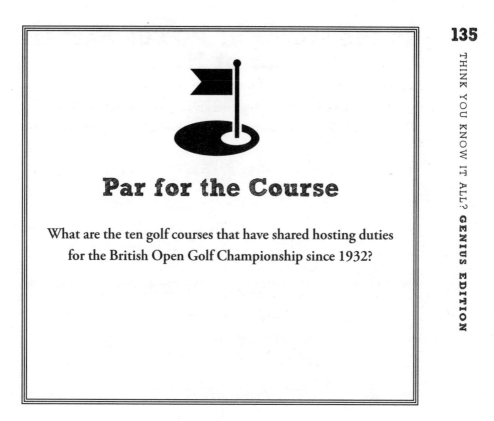

Par for the Course

What are the ten golf courses that have shared hosting duties
for the British Open Golf Championship since 1932?

Four Horsemen

According to the New Testament Book of Revelation, who were
the Four Horsemen of the Apocalypse?

Answers on page 214

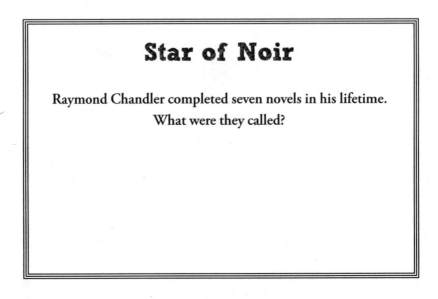

Star of Noir

Raymond Chandler completed seven novels in his lifetime.
What were they called?

A Whale of a Time

What are the six largest whale species?

Answers on page 214

Harrison Ford Movies

Which two of the eight films below does not feature
Harrison Ford?

Witness

Apocalypse Now

Patriot Games

Cape Fear

What Lies Beneath

American Graffiti

Schindler's List

The Call of the Wild

The Need for Speed

As of January 2021, which seven Formula 1 motor racing drivers
had notched up more than thirty Grand Prix wins each?

Answers on pages 214–5

By a Neck

As of 2020, four horses had won the Grand National more than once since 1900. Can you name them all?

Bourne Ready

Can you name the five films released in the Bourne series between 2002 and 2016?

Answers on page 215

A Right Racket

Can you name the twelve women and fourteen men who, as of 2020, had each won five or more Grand Slams in the Open era?

We Three Kings

Who were the three British kings who reigned in 1936?

Answers on page 215

Aping Around

What are the traditional five great apes?

And Cut!

Martin Scorsese has directed feature films that, to 2021, have garnered twenty-nine Oscars in total. Can you recall the eight movies that have won him these ultimate cinematic accolades?

Answers on page 216

Sweeping the Oscars

Which three films have won all the 'Big Five' Oscars (Best Picture, Best Director, Best Actor, Best Actress, Best Screenplay)?

The Stone Age

The Stone Age is often divided into three distinct periods, each with the suffix '-lithic'. Can you remember their names and the order in which they came?

Australian States and Their Capitals

Australia is comprised of eight states and territories.
What are they and, additionally, can you also name their capitals?

Little Women

What are the names of the four March sisters in Louisa May
Alcott's beloved novel, *Little Women*?

The Women of Sex and the City

Can you name the four central characters of the iconic show *Sex and the City* and the actors who played each one?

A Challenge Too Far?

Below is a list of footballers who have competed in the UEFA Champions League. All have won the title at least once, except for two of them. But which two?

Philippe Coutinho

Luis Suárez

Michael Ballack

David Villa

Roberto Baggio

Thierry Henry

Ricardo Carvalho

Rivaldo

Jon Dahl Tomasson

Answers on page 217

♪ World Music ♫

In which countries did each of the following musical genres originate?

A. K-Pop

B. Bossa nova

C. Dancehall

The Poetry of A. A. Milne

Can you remember the titles of A. A. Milne's two volumes of poetry for children?

Answers on page 217

The Works of George Eliot

Mary Ann Evans, better known by her pseudonym
George Eliot, wrote seven novels. What were they?

Born to be Wilde

Oscar Wilde completed seven plays but can you remember
them all?

Answers on page 217

$$E = mc^2$$

It is perhaps the most famous equation in the whole of science, but what do the letters E, m and c represent in Einstein's formulation: $E = mc^2$?

The Novels of Umberto Eco

The Italian thinker and author Umberto Eco published seven novels. What are their titles?

Answers on pages 217–8

Three Men and a Baby

Who were the three male leads in the 1987 movie *Three Men and a Baby?*

Fresh Air

Which seven gases are the major constituents of dry air on Earth?

Answers on page 218

Gassing Away

———◆►◄◆———

Which eleven elements are gasses at room temperature?

A Country Apart

Name the one country in the world whose name contains none of the letters in the word GEOGRAPHY?

Paw Patrol

What are the names of the original seven members of the children's favourite, *Paw Patrol* (one human and six canine)?

Answers on page 218

Darling Children

What are the names of the three 'Darling' children in
J.M. Barrie's Peter Pan?

All in the Eyes

How far can you get with labelling the constituent parts on this
diagram of a human eye?

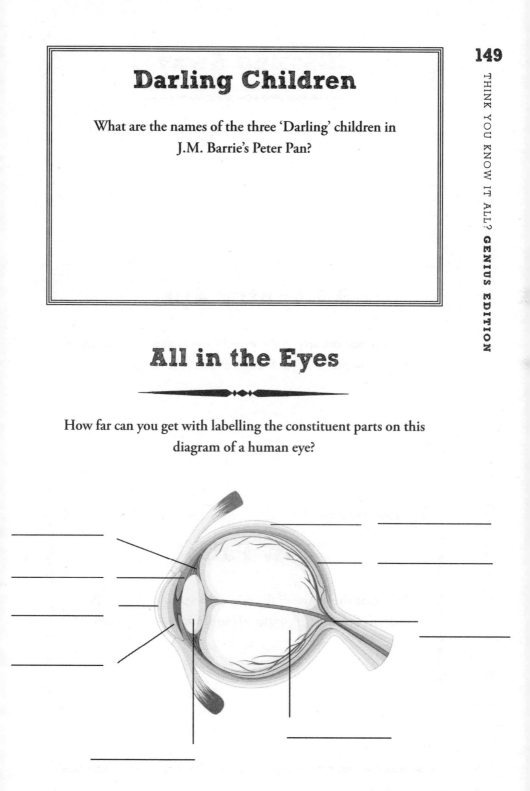

Answers on page 219

FEELING CONFIDENT?

LET'S SEE HOW WELL YOU'VE DONE ...

THE ANSWERS

A RIVER RUNS THROUGH IT

Burundi
The Democratic
   Republic of the Congo
Egypt
Eritrea
Ethiopia
Kenya
Rwanda
South Sudan
Sudan
Tanzania
Uganda

NAME THE AUTHOR

A. Charles Darwin
B. Albert Einstein
C. Richard Dawkins
D. Carl Sagan
E. Rachel Carson
F. Dian Fossey
G. James Lovelock

KEEPING COMPOSED

A. George Gershwin
B. Sara Bareilles
C. Andrew Lloyd Webber
D. Lin-Manuel Miranda
E. Alan Menken
F. Stephen Sondheim
G. Claude-Michel Schönberg
H. Richard O'Brien
I. John Kander
J. Richard Rodgers

BORDER CHECKS PART I

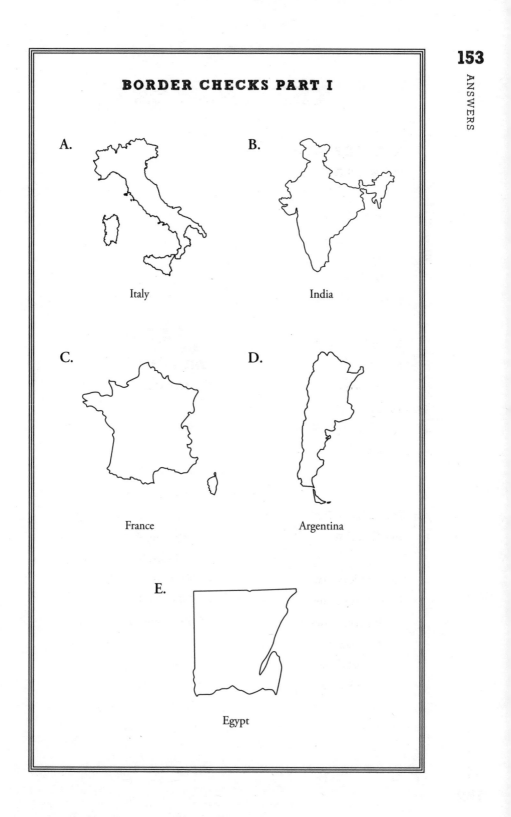

A.

Italy

B.

India

C.

France

D.

Argentina

E.

Egypt

TASTE SENSATIONS

Bitter
Salty
Sour
Sweet
Umami

LEND ME YOUR EARS

Friends, Romans and
  countrymen

SOUTH AMERICAN STATES

Argentina
Bolivia
Brazil
Chile
Colombia
Ecuador
Guyana
Paraguay
Peru
Suriname
Uruguay
Venezuela

MOONS OF THE SOLAR SYSTEM

Ganymede
Titan
Callisto
Io
Moon
Europa
Triton

BOND THEME SONGS

A. Tom Jones
B. Paul McCartney & Wings
C. Lulu
D. Carly Simon
E. Shirley Bassey
F. Sheena Easton
G. Rita Coolidge
H. Duran Duran
I. A-ha
J. Gladys Knight
K. Tina Turner
L. Sheryl Crow
M. Garbage

N. Madonna

O. Chris Cornell

P. Jack White and Alicia Keys

Q. Adele

R. Sam Smith

S. Billie Eilish

THE HORCRUX OF THE MATTER

Tom Riddle's Diary

Marvolo Gaunt's Ring

Salazar Slytherin's Locket

Helga Hufflepuff's Cup

Rowena Ravenclaw's Diadem

Nagini the Snake

Harry Potter himself

THE LANGUAGE OF DIPLOMACY

Arabic

Chinese (Mandarin, with
  simplified characters)

English

French

Russian

Spanish

PREMIER LEAGUE CHAMPIONS

Arsenal

Blackburn Rovers

Chelsea

Leicester City

Liverpool

Manchester City

Manchester United

IN VOGUE

Fred Astaire

Lauren Bacall

Marlon Brando

Bette Davis

Jimmy Dean

Marlene Dietrich

Joe DiMaggio

Greta Garbo

Jean Harlow

Rita Hayworth

Katherine Hepburn

Marilyn Monroe

Gene Kelly

Grace Kelly

Ginger Rogers

Lana Turner

INTERNATIONAL LEADERS PART I

A. Jacinda Arden
B. Narendra Modi
C. Emmanuel Macron
D. Greta Thunberg
E. Xi Jinping

THE MAGNIFICENT SEVEN

A. Yul Brynner
B. Steve McQueen
C. Charles Bronson
D. Robert Vaughn
E. Horst Buchholz
F. James Coburn
G. Brad Dexter

WORLD CUP GOLDEN BOOT WINNERS

1982 Paolo Rossi (Italy)
1986 Gary Lineker (England)
1990 Salvatore Schillaci (Italy)
1994 Oleg Salenko (Russia)
/ Hristo Stoichkov
(Bulgaria) (joint winners)
1998 Davor Šuker (Croatia)
2002 Ronaldo (Brazil)
2006 Miroslav Klose (Germany)
2010 Thomas Müller (Germany)
2014 James Rodríguez
(Colombia)
2018 Harry Kane (England)

WHO'S IN THE BAND?

New Kids on the Block
Joey McIntyre
Jonathan Knight
Jordan Knight
Donnie Wahlberg
Danny Wood

The Spice Girls
Victoria Adams (Posh)
Melanie Brown (Mel B; Scary)
Emma Bunton (Baby)
Melanie Chisholm (Mel C;
Sporty)
Geri Halliwell (Ginger)

Destiny's Child
Beyoncé Knowles
Kelly Rowland
Michelle Williams

CURRENCIES OF THE WORLD

A. Afghani
B. Ruble
C. Boliviano
D. Koruna
E. Krone
F. Dalasi
G. Forint
H. Dinar
I. Shekel
J. Shilling
K. Ringgit
L. Rupee
M. Dirham
N. Cordoba
O. Won
P. Zloty
Q. Riyal
R. Baht
S. Lira
T. Dong

VOLCANOES

United States (173 volcanoes)
Russia (166)
Indonesia (139)
Iceland (130)

Japan (112)
Chile (104)
Ethiopia (57)
Papua New Guinea (53)
Philippines (50)
Mexico (43)

SHERLOCK HOLMES NOVELS

A Study in Scarlet
The Sign of the Four
The Hound of the Baskervilles
The Valley of Fear

THE KENTUCKY DERBY

Lincoln's Cigar and Startled Charlie

SCREEN LEGEND

Alfred Hitchcock

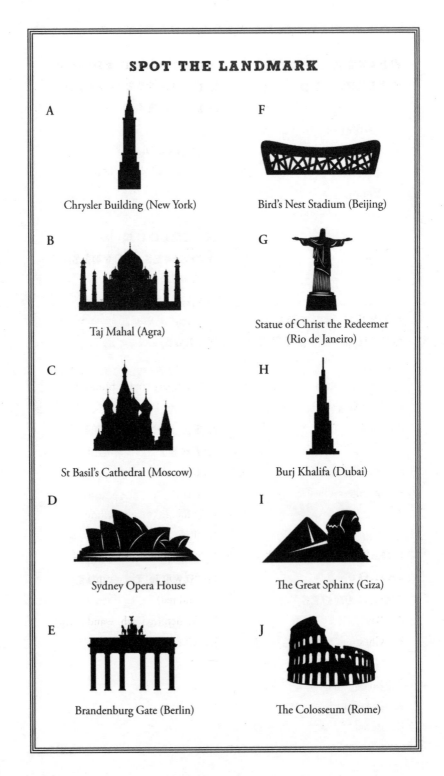

SPOT THE LANDMARK

A
Chrysler Building (New York)

B
Taj Mahal (Agra)

C
St Basil's Cathedral (Moscow)

D
Sydney Opera House

E
Brandenburg Gate (Berlin)

F
Bird's Nest Stadium (Beijing)

G
Statue of Christ the Redeemer
(Rio de Janeiro)

H
Burj Khalifa (Dubai)

I
The Great Sphinx (Giza)

J
The Colosseum (Rome)

WHICH WITCH IS WHICH?

A. Harry Potter
B. The Wicked Witch of the East
C. Merlin
D. The Three Witches of *Macbeth*
E. Gandalf

IN THE WORDS OF POTUS PART I

A. Jimmy Carter
B. Dwight D. Eisenhower
C. Bill Clinton
D. Gerald Ford
E. Donald Trump
F. George W. Bush

COATS OF MANY COLOURS

A. Bay
B. Chestnut
C. Grey
D. Palamino
E. Skewbald
F. Piebald

THOSE MAGNIFICENT MEN IN THEIR FLYING MACHINES

A. Louis Blériot
B. Major Frederick Martin
C. Richard E. Byrd and Floyd Bennett
D. Charles Lindbergh
E. Richard E. Byrd and Bernt Balchen

FLAGS

A. Hungary (red, white and green)
B. Bangladesh (red on green)
C. Albania (black on red)
D. Nigeria (green, white and green)
E. Finland (blue on white)
F. Russia (white, blue and red)
G. Singapore (red and white)
H. Kuwait (black, green, white and red)
I. Yemen (red, white and black)
J. Ukraine (blue and gold)

SHAKESPEARE'S OPENING LINES

A. *Macbeth*
B. *Richard III*
C. *Henry V*
D. *As You Like It*
E. *Henry IV, Pt 1*
F. *All's Well That Ends Well*
G. *Titus Andronicus*
H. *Twelfth Night*
I. *Romeo and Juliet*
J. *Antony and Cleopatra*

ALL ROMAN TO ME

A. Gallia
B. Africa
C. Dacia
D. Helvetia
E. Hibernia
F. Hispania
G. Phoenicia

CHURCH AND STATE

John F. Kennedy and Joe Biden

CHAMPS

Gerhard Berger and Stirling Moss

NOVEL NUMBERS

A. *1984*
B. *84, Charing Cross Road*
C. *A Thousand Splendid Suns*
D. *The Big Four*
E. *Around the World in Eighty Days*
F. *Fahrenheit 451*
G. *One Hundred Years of Solitude*
H. *Slaughterhouse-Five*
I. *The Five People You Meet in Heaven*
J. *The House of the Seven Gables*

SI PREFIXES

A. Mega
B. Giga
C. Tera
D. Peta
E. Exa
F. Zetta
G. Yotta

BEATLES US NO. 1S

A Hard Day's Night
All You Need is Love
Can't Buy Me Love
Come Together
Eight Days a Week
Get Back
Hello Goodbye
Help!
Hey Jude
I Feel Fine
I Want to Hold Your Hand
Let it Be
Love Me Do
Paperback Writer
Penny Lane
She Loves You
The Long and Winding Road/
    For You Blue
Ticket to Ride
We Can Work It Out
Yesterday

SPORTS GROUNDS

A. Fenway Park
B. Ibrox Stadium
C. Estadio Monumental Antonio
    Vespucio Liberti (a.k.a.
    Monumental de Nuñez)
D. Stadio Giuseppe Meazza
    (a.k.a. the San Siro)
E. The Maracanã
F. Santiago Bernabéu
G. Madison Square Garden
H. Wrigley Field
I. The Gabba
J. FNB Stadium (a.k.a. Soccer
    City / The Calabash)

WHO WAS WHO IN GAME OF THRONES?

A. Margaery Tyrell
B. Robert Baratheon
C. Jaime Lannister
D. Daenerys Targaryen
E. Eddard 'Ned' Stark
F. Jorah Mormont
G. Arya Stark
H. Theon Greyjoy
I. Jeor Mormont
J. Tywin Lannister

BORDER CHECKS PART II

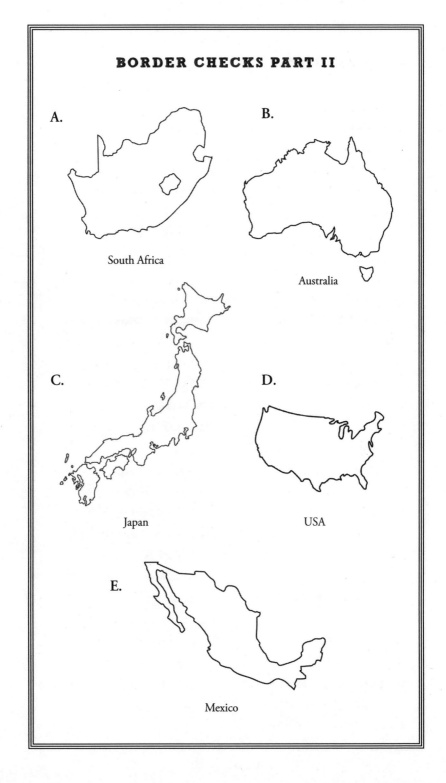

A.

South Africa

B.

Australia

C.

Japan

D.

USA

E.

Mexico

PAPAL NAMES

A. John Paul II
B. Paul VI
C. Benedict XVI
D. Pius XI
E. Pius XII
F. John XXIII
G. Francis
H. John Paul I

THE CAR'S THE STAR

A. Austin-Healey
B. Volkswagen
C. Cadillac
D. Citroën
E. MG
F. Mazda
G. Fiat
H. Honda
I. Toyota
J. Jaguar
K. Nissan
L. Jeep
M. Lotus
N. Maserati
O. Ford
P. Porsche
Q. Alfa Romeo
R. Dodge
S. Mitsubishi
T. Buick

I LIKE TO RIDE MY BICYCLE

Giro d'Italia
Tour de France
Vuelta a España

DINGBATS PART I

Taylor Swift
Neil Armstrong
Bill Gates

THE ANIMALS OF BEATRIX POTTER

A. Hedgehog
B. Badger
C. Frog
D. Toad
E. Fox
F. Mole
G. Cat

H. Squirrel
I. Mouse
J. Rat
K. Rabbit
L. Pig

RAFFLE WINNER

Singapore Sling

ON BRAND

A. Nike
B. Samsung
C. Hyundai
D. Nivea
E. Reebok
F. Jagermeister
G. Lego
H. Volkswagen
I. Adidas
J. Spar
K. Volvo

INTERNATIONAL LEADERS PART II

A. Angela Merkel
B. Kamala Harris
C. Justin Trudeau
D. Ursula von der Leyen
E. Cyril Rampahosa

REIGNING MONARCHS

A. Belgium
B. Saudi Arabia
C. Sweden
D. Bhutan
E. Liechtenstein
F. Norway
G. Tonga
H. Spain
I. Cambodia
J. Jordan
K. Monaco
L. Lesotho
M. Denmark
N. Morocco
O. Netherlands

COLOURFUL STORIES

A. Nathaniel Hawthorne

B. Chimamanda Ngozi Adichie

C. Stephen King

D. Anthony Burgess

E. Philip Pullman

F. Toni Morrison

G. Alice Walker

H. Anna Sewell

I. Aravind Adiga

J. E. L. James

THE REGIONS OF ITALY

Lombardy

Valle D'Aosta

Piedmont

Liguris

Tuscany

Umbria

Lazio

Sardinia

Campania

Sicily

Trentino-Alto Adige

Eriuli-Venezia Giulia

Veneto

Bologna

Marche

Abruzzo

Molise

Puglia

Basilicata

Calabria

A SPORTING CHANCE

A. Ice hockey
B. Australian Rules Football
C. Baseball
D. Cricket
E. Rugby League
F. Basketball
G. Football (soccer)
H. American Football
I. Rugby Union

POETRY TO MY EARS

A. Alexander Pope
B. Percy Bysshe Shelley
C. Emily Dickinson
D. W. B. Yeats
E. Lewis Carroll
F. William Wordsworth
G. Alfred, Lord Tennyson
H. Gertrude Stein
I. William Ernest Henley
J. Ogden Nash
K. John McCrae
L. John Keats
M. Sylvia Plath
N. T. S. Eliot

O. W. H. Auden
P. Maya Angelou
Q. Dylan Thomas
R. Robert Frost
S. Samuel Taylor Coleridge
T. Elizabeth Barrett Browning

THE NEED FOR SPEED

A. Australia
B. France
C. Italy
D. Germany
E. Mexico
F. Austria
G. USA
H. Japan
I. Portugal
J. Argentina
K. Malaysia
L. South Africa
M. Netherlands
N. Canada
O. Brazil
P. Belgium

ANIMAL ART

Horses

ACTING OUT

A. Freddie Mercury

B. Edith Piaf

C. June Carter Cash

D. Ray Charles

E. Winston Churchill

F. Queen Anne

G. Ábraham Lincoln

H. Margaret Thatcher

I. King George VI

J. Harvey Milk

K. Idi Amin

L. Queen Elizabeth II

M. Truman Capote

N. Virginia Woolf

O. Lee Krasner

P. Stephen Hawking

Q. Erin Brockovich

UP TO THE OCKEY

A ROSE BY ANY OTHER NAME

A. Alice Cooper
B. Michael Caine
C. John Wayne
D. Slash
E. Nicki Minaj
F. Katy Perry
G. Pink

H. The Edge
I. Sade
J. 50 Cent
K. Snoop Dogg
L. Alicia Keys
M. Shania Twain
N. LL Cool J
O. Iggy Pop
P. Lana Del Rey

ALL HAIL THE BRAILLE

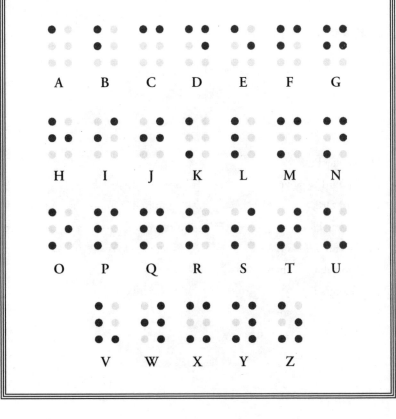

OFF THE SCALE

A. Risk of death
B. The comparative strength of chess players
C. Consciousness
D. Electrical resistance
E. Chilli heat
F. Purchasing power parity
G. The height of horses
H. Luminous intensity
I. Amount of substance
J. Thermodynamic temperature

NAME THAT TUNESMITH

A. Giacomo Puccini
B. Edvard Grieg
C. Antonio Vivaldi
D. Samuel Barber
E. Richard Wagner
F. Carl Orff
G. Gustav Holst
H. Johann Strauss II
I. Pyotr Ilyich Tchaikovsky
J. Georges Bizet
K. Wolfgang Amadeus Mozart
L. Gioachino Rossini
M. Bedřich Smetana

N. George Frideric Handel
O. Gabriel Fauré
P. Johann Strauss I
Q. Ludwig van Beethoven
R. Sergei Rachmaninoff

MONA LISA

A. Leonardo da Vinci
B. *La Gioconda*
C. Lisa Gherardini
D. Napoleon
E. The Louvre in Paris
F. He notoriously stole it from the Louvre in 1911

TOP OF THE PUCKS

Montreal Canadiens (24 cups)
Toronto Maple Leafs (13)
Detroit Red Wings (11)
Boston Bruins (6)
Chicago Blackhawks (6)
Edmonton Oilers (5)
Pittsburgh Penguins (5)

MIXED-UP COUNTRIES

A. Mongolia
B. Algeria
C. Montenegro
D. Macedonia
E. Suriname
F. Israel
G. Germany
H. Iceland
I. El Salvador
J. Laos
K. Singapore
L. Yemen
M. Micronesia
N. Oman
O. Honduras
P. Cote d'Ivoire
Q. Nepal
R. Switzerland
S. Cameroon
T. Belarus

RUGBY WORLD CUP-WINNING CAPTAINS

A. David Kirk
B. Nick Farr-Jones
C. Francois Pienaar
D. John Eales
E. Martin Johnson
F. John Smit
G. Richie McCaw
H. Richie McCaw
I. Siya Kolisi

A CAPITAL IDEA

Pretoria (administrative);
Cape Town (legislative);
Bloemfontein (judicial)

PICTURE THIS!

Paul Revere's ride in 1775, during the American Revolutionary War. It was famously the subject of an eponymous poem by Henry Wadsworth Longfellow.

HUNGRY FOR KNOWLEDGE

The Hunger Games; Catching Fire; Mockingjay; The Ballad of Songbirds and Snakes

THE STATES OF THE NATION

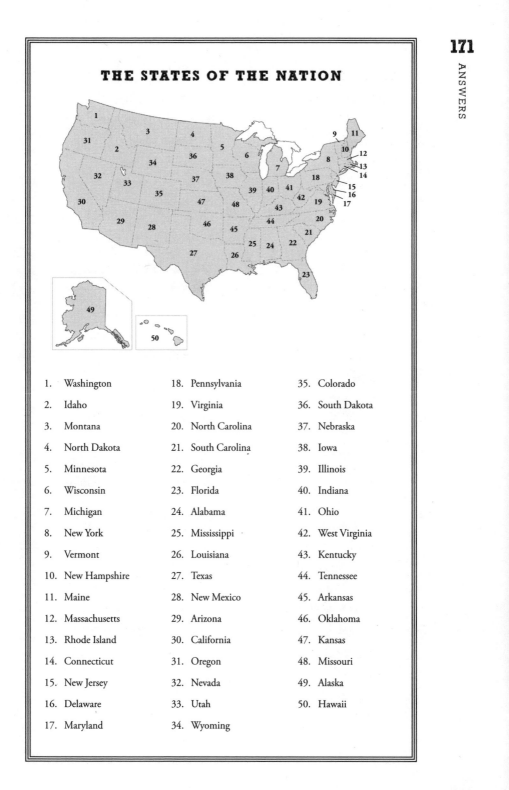

1. Washington	18. Pennsylvania	35. Colorado
2. Idaho	19. Virginia	36. South Dakota
3. Montana	20. North Carolina	37. Nebraska
4. North Dakota	21. South Carolina	38. Iowa
5. Minnesota	22. Georgia	39. Illinois
6. Wisconsin	23. Florida	40. Indiana
7. Michigan	24. Alabama	41. Ohio
8. New York	25. Mississippi	42. West Virginia
9. Vermont	26. Louisiana	43. Kentucky
10. New Hampshire	27. Texas	44. Tennessee
11. Maine	28. New Mexico	45. Arkansas
12. Massachusetts	29. Arizona	46. Oklahoma
13. Rhode Island	30. California	47. Kansas
14. Connecticut	31. Oregon	48. Missouri
15. New Jersey	32. Nevada	49. Alaska
16. Delaware	33. Utah	50. Hawaii
17. Maryland	34. Wyoming	

SWIFTLY TO THE POINT

Taylor Swift
Fearless
Speak Now
Red
1989
Reputation
Lover
Folklore
Evermore

NOISES OFF

A. Justin Timberlake
B. Dakota Fanning
C. Robin Williams
D. Mila Kunis
E. Matthew Broderick
F. Samuel L. Jackson
G. Dan Castellaneta
H. Ellen de Generes

I. Michael J. Fox
J. Oprah Winfrey
K. Scarlett Johansson
L. Orson Welles
M. Cameron Diaz
N. John Goodman
O. Angelina Jolie

GULLIVER'S TRAVELS

Lilliput
Brobdingnag
Laputa
Balnibarbi
Luggnagg
Glubbdubdrib
Japan
The Land of the Houyhnhnms

PASTA VARIETIES

A. Penne

B. Orecchiette

C. Conchiglie

D. Cavatappi

E. Fusilli

F. Farfalle

G. Macaroni

H. Rigatoni

I. Lasagne

J. Cannelloni

K. Pappardelle

L. Ravioli

M. Bucatini

N. Ruote

O. Pipe Rigate

ON THE RECORD

A. Bob Dylan

B. Jefferson Airplane

C. Cream

D. Creedence Clearwater Revival

E. Pink Floyd

F. Aerosmith

G. Bruce Springsteen

H. Neil Young & Crazy Horse

I. ZZ Top

J. Queen

K. Bon Jovi

L. Def Leppard

M. U2

N. Foo Fighters

O. Queens of the Stone Age

P. The White Stripes

Q. Green Day

R. Kings of Leon

S. The Black Keys

T. Arctic Monkeys

U. David Bowie

BEST OF ENEMIES

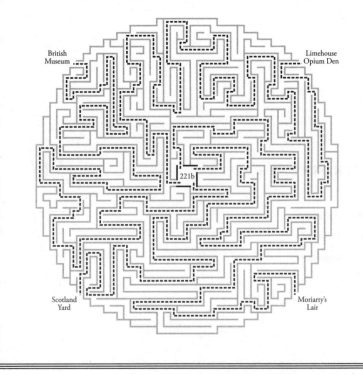

FAMOUS LAST WORDS PART I

A. *The Great Gatsby*
   (F. Scott Fitzgerald)
B. *Gone with the Wind*
   (Margaret Mitchell)
C. *To Kill a Mockingbird*
   (Harper Lee)
D. *The Bell Jar* (Sylvia Plath)
E. *Animal Farm* (George Orwell)
F. *Life of Pi* (Yann Martel)
G. *The Catcher in the Rye*
   (J. D. Salinger)
H. *A Tale of Two Cities*
   (Charles Dickens)

WELL BREAD

Seaweed

DINOSAURS PART I

A. *Triceratops*
B. *Ankylosaurus*
C. *Stegosaurus*
D. *Coelophysis*
E. *Tyrannosaurus rex*

THE SUM TOTAL

78 (39 x 2)

SOMETHING TO GET YOUR TEETH INTO

A. Canine
———————

B. Premolar
———————

C. Molar
———————

D. Incisor
———————

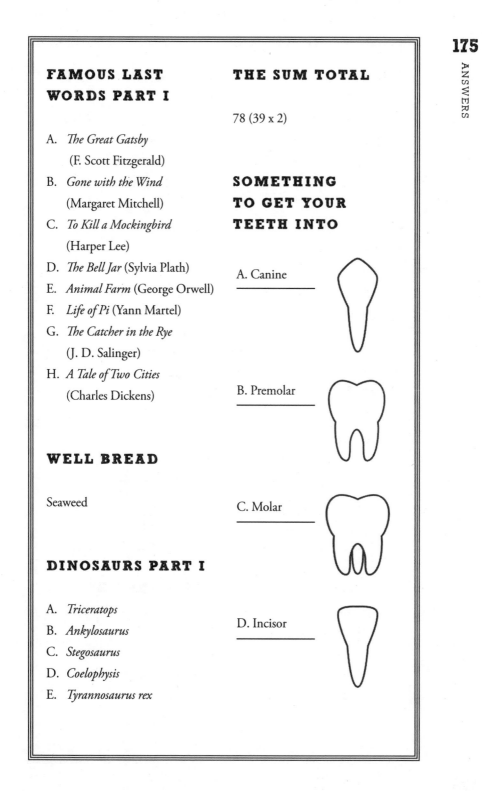

WHERE THE HEART IS

A. Belgium
B. Iceland
C. Brazil
D. Colombia
E. New Zealand
F. Cuba
G. Barbados
H. Haiti
I. Senegal
J. Mexico

HIT FOR SIX

Most test runs:
Sachin Tendulkar
Ricky Ponting
Jacques Kallis
Rahul Dravid
Alastair Cook

Most test wickets:
Muttiah Muralitharan
Shane Warne
Anil Kumble
James Anderson
Glenn McGrath

WORLD CUP HOSTS

A. Montevideo (Uruguay)
B. Rome (Italy)
C. Paris (France)
D. Rio de Janeiro (Brazil)
E. Bern (Switzerland)
F. Solna (Sweden)
G. Santiago (Chile)
H. London (England)
I. Mexico City (Mexico)
J. Munich (West Germany)
K. Buenos Aires (Argentina)
L. Madrid (Spain)
M. Mexico City (Mexico)
N. Rome (Italy)
O. Pasadena (USA)
P. Saint-Denis (France)
Q. Yokohama (Japan)
R. Berlin (Germany)
S. Johannesburg (South Africa)
T. Rio de Janeiro (Brazil)
U. Moscow (Russia)

THE WORKS OF JAMES JOYCE

Dubliners, A Portrait of the Artist as a Young Man, Ulysses, Finnegans Wake

CONSTELLATIONS

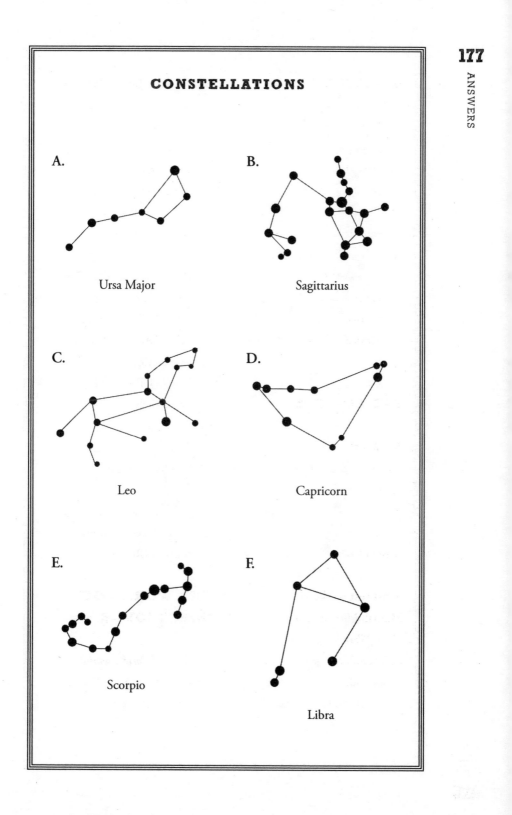

A.

Ursa Major

B.

Sagittarius

C.

Leo

D.

Capricorn

E.

Scorpio

F.

Libra

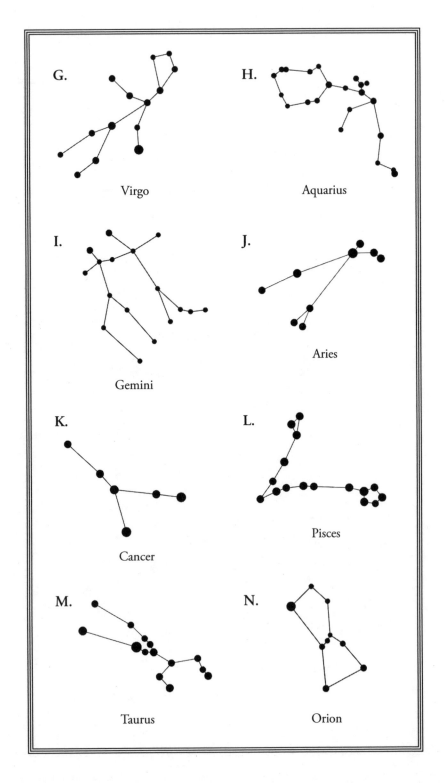

G.

Virgo

H.

Aquarius

I.

Gemini

J.

Aries

K.

Cancer

L.

Pisces

M.

Taurus

N.

Orion

A PRIME EXAMPLE

31, 37, 41, 43, 47, 53, 59, 61, 67, 71, 73, 79, 83, 89, 97, 101, 103, 107, 109 and 113

SLAM DUNK

Los Angeles Lakers
(including time as
Minneapolis Lakers) (17)
Boston Celtics (17)
Golden State Warriors
(including time as
Philadelphia and San
Francisco Warriors) (6)
Chicago Bulls (6)
San Antonio Spurs (5)
Philadelphia 76ers (including
time as Syracuse Nationals) (3)
Detroit Pistons (including time
as Fort Wayne Pistons) (3)
Miami Heat (3)
New York Knicks (2)
Houston Rockets (2)

THE TOP JOB

John Tyler
Millard Fillmore
Andrew Johnson
Chester A. Arthur
Theodore Roosevelt
Calvin Coolidge
Harry S. Truman
Lyndon B. Johnson
Gerald Ford

BOGIE AND BACALL

To Have and Have Not
The Big Sleep
Dark Passage
Key Largo

SPOT THE DIFFERENCE

THE WORKS OF DONNA TARTT

The Secret History
The Little Friend
The Goldfinch

WHEN THE CAPE IS OFF

A. Steven (Steve) Rogers
B. Selina Kyle
C. Robert Louis (Bobby) Drake
D. Britt Reid
E. Bruce Banner
F. Tony Stark
G. Max Eisenhardt
H. Reed Richards
I. Dick Grayson
J. Kara Danvers (born Kara Zor-El)
K. Benjamin Grimm
L. Diana Prince

THE ANTAGONISTS OF ROCKY

A. Apollo Creed
B. Apollo Creed
C. James 'Clubber' Lang
D. Ivan Drago
E. Tommy Gunn
F. Mason 'The Line' Dixon
G. 'Pretty' Ricky Conlan
H. Viktor Drago

DE NIRO AND PACINO

The Godfather Part II
Heat
Righteous Kill
The Irishman

MIXED-UP CELEBS

A. Meg Ryan
B. Russell Crowe
C. Britney Spears
D. Emma Watson
E. Ryan Gosling
F. Clint Eastwood
G. Drew Barrymore
H. Eric Clapton
I. Jennifer Aniston
J. John Mayer
K. Gillian Anderson
L. Bruce Springsteen

NAME THAT ARTIST PART I

A. *Monet Family in Their Argenteuil Garden* by Edouard Manet
B. *Women Picking Olives* by Vincent van Gogh
C. *Madame X* by John Singer Sargent
D. *Young Woman Braiding her Hair* by Auguste Renoir

MUSICAL MATHS

98 (3 x 50 – 52)

HARD CHEESE

Rennet

ALL IN THE MIND

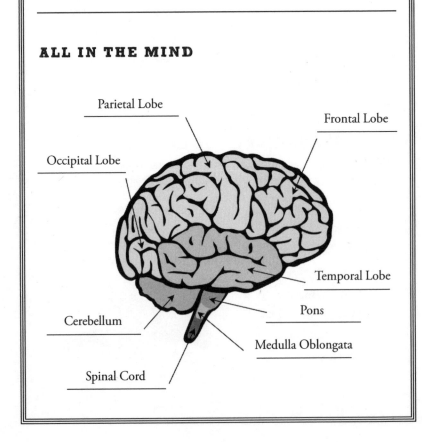

Parietal Lobe

Frontal Lobe

Occipital Lobe

Temporal Lobe

Pons

Cerebellum

Medulla Oblongata

Spinal Cord

THE HELPLESS SHAH

Chess

GILBERT AND SULLIVAN

A. *H.M.S. Pinafore*
B. *Iolanthe*
C. *Ruddigore*
D. *Trial by Jury*
E. *The Mikado*
F. *The Sorcerer*
G. *Patience*
H. *Pirates of Penzance*
I. *Princess Ida*
J. *The Gondoliers*
K. *The Yeomen of the Guard*

LITTLE BUT PERFECTLY FORMED

Ceres, Eris, Haumea, Pluto, Makemake

DINGBATS PART II

A. Judy Garland
B. Donald Trump
C. Brad Pitt

DON QUIXOTE

Sancho Panza

WHO'S ON FIRST BASE?

1. Pitcher
2. Catcher
3. First Base
4. Second Base
5. Third Base
6. Short Stop
7. Left Field
8. Centre Field
9. Right Field

AFRICA'S CAPITALS

A. Luanda
B. Porto-Novo
C. Ouagadougou
D. Kinshasa
E. Brazzaville
F. Asmara
G. Libreville
H. Maseru
I. Monrovia
J. Linlongwe
K. Rabat
L. Windhoek
M. Abuja
N. Kigali
O. Dakar
P. Mogadishu
Q. Dodoma
R. Lomé
S. Kampala
T. Lusaka

HARD TO CATEGORISE

Domain
Kingdom
Phylum
Class
Order
Family
Genus
Species

LITERARY LOVERS

A. *Brokeback Mountain* (Anne Proulx)
B. *Love in the Time of Cholera* (Gabriel Garcia Marquez)
C. *The Time Traveler's Wife* (Audrey Niffenegger)
D. *Wuthering Heights* (Emily Brontë)
E. *The Fault in Our Stars* (John Green)
F. *The Hunger Games* (Suzanne Collins)
G. *Love Story* (Erich Segal)
H. *Lady Chatterley's Lover* (D. H. Lawrence)
I. *The Sun Also Rises* (Ernest Hemingway)

SPORTING TERMS

Trampolining

AN ODYSSEY THROUGH HOMER

A. Penelope
B. Telemachus
C. Eumaeus
D. Calypso
E. Circe
F. Athena
G. Laertes
H. Nestor
I. Menelaus
J. Helen

THE LEAGUE OF EXTRAORDINARY GENTLEMEN

A. Allan Quartermain
B. Captain Nemo
C. Mina Harker
D. Dorian Gray
E. Tom Sawyer
F. Dr Henry Jekyll / Edward Hyde
G. Ishmael

SOUNDS ABOUT RIGHT

A. Malleus (or hammer)
B. Incus (or anvil)
C. Stapes (or stirrup)

ROYAL LOVE

A. Catherine the Great
B. Napoleon III
C. Charles II
D. Louis XV
E. George IV
F. Edward VIII
G. Napoleon I
H. Louis XIV
I. Edward VII
J. Peter the Great

AMAZING AMAZON

Brazil
Colombia
Peru

INDIAN CUISINE

A. Aloo
B. Dal
C. Gobi
D. Murgh
E. Sag
F. Lassi
G. Gosht

SHAKESPEAREAN CHARACTERS

A. *Much Ado About Nothing*
B. *The Tempest*
C. *Romeo and Juliet*
D. *The Merchant of Venice*
E. *As You Like It*
F. *The Taming of the Shrew*
G. *Othello*
H. *Troilus and Cressida*
I. *Antony and Cleopatra*
J. *The Merry Wives of Windsor*
K. *Measure for Measure*
L. *Twelfth Night*

THREE SIDES TO EVERY STORY

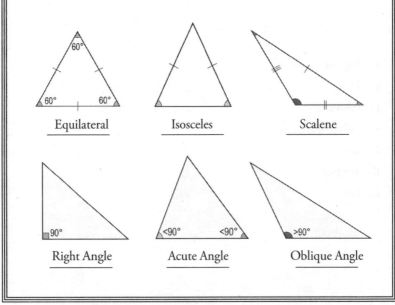

Equilateral

Isosceles

Scalene

Right Angle

Acute Angle

Oblique Angle

HOME RUN!

Barry Bonds (762 home runs)

Hank Aaron (755)

Babe Ruth (714)

Alex Rodriguez (696)

Albert Pujols (662)

Willie Mays (660)

Ken Griffey, Jr. (630)

Jim Thome (612)

Sammy Sosa (609)

Frank Robinson (586)

IN BLOOM

A. African Violet

B. Anthurium

C. Bird of Paradise

D. Calla Lily

E. Cyclamen

F. Daffodil

G. Daisy

H. Gladiola

I. Hibiscus

J. Iris

K. Jasmine

L. Lily

M. Rose

N. Sunflower

O. Tulip

PRIX DE L'ARC DE TRIOMPHE

Longchamp

CLASSICAL CLASSICS

A. Suetonius

B. Euripides

C. Sun Tzu

D. Plato

E. Ovid

F. Sophocles

G. Aristophanes

H. Petronius

I. Homer

J. Virgil

K. Aeschylus

L. Krishna-Dwaipayana Vyasa

M. Tacitus

YOGA POSITIONS

A.

Sphinx

B.

Cat Pose

C.

Warrior

D.

Chair Pose

E.

Cow Pose

F.

Cobra

G.

Hero

H.

Downward Dog

WHO'S ON DRUMS?

Guns N' Roses
Izzy Stradlin
Steven Adler
Axl Rose
Duff McKagan
Slash

The Who
Roger Daltrey
Pete Townshend
John Entwistle
Keith Moon

Fleetwood Mac
Mick Fleetwood
John McVie
Christine McVie
Lindsey Buckingham
Stevie Nicks

REM
Bill Berry
Peter Buck
Mike Mills
Michael Stipe

The Police
Sting
Stewart Copeland
Henry Padovani
Andy Summers

Nirvana
Kurt Cobain
Krist Novoselic
Dave Grohl

SINGLE-TERM PRESIDENTS

John Adams
John Quincy Adams
Martin Van Buren
Franklin Pierce
Grover Cleveland
Benjamin Harrison
William Howard Taft
Herbert Hoover
Gerald Ford
Jimmy Carter
George H. W. Bush
Donald Trump

ON CLOUD CANINE

A. Rin Tin Tin
B. Dash
C. Charley
D. Greyfriars Bobby
E. Uggie (*The Artist*)
F. Marley
G. Nipper
H. Pickles

CAUGHT RED-HANDED

A. Loop
B. Whorl
C. Arch

NEXT DOOR TO RUSSIA

Azerbaijan
Belarus
China
Estonia
Finland
Georgia
Kazakhstan
Latvia
Lithuania
Mongolia
North Korea
Norway
Poland
Ukraine

ELEMENTARY, MY DEAR QUIZZER

Abbreviation	Element name	Person
Gd	Gadolinium	Johan Gadolin
Cm	Curium	Marie Curie and Pierre Curie
Bk	Berkelium	George Berkeley
Es	Einsteinium	Albert Einstein
Fm	Fermium	Enrico Fermi
Md	Mendelevium	Dmitri Mendeleev
No	Nobelium	Alfred Nobel
Lr	Lawrencium	Ernest Lawrence
Rf	Rutherfordium	Ernest Rutherford
Bh	Bohrium	Niels Bohr
Mt	Meitnerium	Lise Meitner
Rg	Roentgenium	Wilhelm Röntgen
Cn	Copernicium	Nicolaus Copernicus
Lv	Livermorium	Robert Livermore
Og	Oganesson	Yuri Oganessian

WHAT THE DICKENS?

A. *Bleak House*
B. *The Mystery of Edwin Drood*
C. *Our Mutual Friend*
D. *Little Dorrit*
E. *Martin Chuzzlewit*
F. *Great Expectations*
G. *The Pickwick Papers*
H. *The Chimes*
I. *A Tale of Two Cities*
J. *Oliver Twist*
K. *The Mudfog Papers*
L. *A Christmas Carol*
M. *Hard Times*
N. *Nicholas Nickleby*
O. *David Copperfield*

KAFKA-ESQUE

The Trial
The Castle
Amerika

IS IT A BIRD, IS IT A PLANE?

A. George Reeves
B. Christopher Reeve
C. John Haymes Newton
D. Gerard Christopher
E. Dean Cain
F. Tom Welling
G. Brandon Routh
H. Henry Cavill

IN TUNE

A. Semibreve (1 whole note)
B. Minim (1/2)
C. Crotchet (1/4)
D. Quaver (1/8)
E. Semiquaver (1/16)
F. Demisemiquaver (1/32)
G. Hemidemisemiquaver (1/64)

THE CHARACTERS OF FROZEN

A. Elsa
B. Anna
C. Olaf
D. Kristoff

E. Sven

F. Hans

G. Oaken

H. Grand Pabbie

I. Marshmallow

C. John Bellingham

D. Lee Harvey Oswald

E. Leon Czolgosz

F. Mijailo Mijailović

G. Nathuram Godse

H. Thenmozhi Rajaratnam

ASSASSINS

A. Gavrilo Princip

B. James Earl Ray

MUSICAL RIVALS

Salieri

FLOWER POWER

CHAMPION OF CHAMPIONS

Real Madrid (13 titles)
AC Milan (7)
Bayern Munich (6)
Liverpool (6)
Barcelona (5)
Ajax (4)
Inter Milan (3)
Manchester United (3)
Juventus (2)
Benfica (2)
Nottingham Forest (2)
Porto (2)

MISS MARPLE

The Murder at the Vicarage
The Body in the Library
The Moving Finger
A Murder Is Announced
They Do It with Mirrors
A Pocket Full of Rye
4.50 from Paddington
The Mirror Crack'd from Side to Side
A Caribbean Mystery
At Bertram's Hotel
Nemesis
Sleeping Murder

CRACKING THE LATIN CODE

Sums: 3, 15, 191, 18, 919, 45, 14
Numeric code: 3/1/5/19/1/18
9/19 4/5/1/4
Message: CAESAR IS DEAD

I LIKE YOUR STYLE

A. Cubism
B. Pointillism
C. Pop art
D. Art nouveau

A WHOLE LOT OF HISTORY

A. 753 BC
B. 332 BC
C. AD 312

D. AD 800
E. 1215
F. 1453
G. 1492
H. 1564
I. 1687
J. 1789
K. 1859
L. 1893
M. 1905
N. 1917
O. 1949
P. 1989
Q. 1994

STANS OF THE WORLD

Afghanistan
Kazakhstan
Kyrgyzstan
Pakistan
Tajikistan
Turkmenistan
Uzbekistan

DISNEY ANTHEMS

A. *Moana*
B. *Jungle Book*
C. *The Little Mermaid*
D. *Frozen II*
E. *Dumbo*
F. *Mary Poppins*
G. *Pinocchio*
H. *Coco*
I. *Aladdin*
J. *Lady and the Tramp*
K. *The Lion King*
L. *Beauty and the Beast*
M. *Tangled*
N. *Cinderella*
O. *Toy Story*

A ROCK AND A HARD PLACE

Sedimentary
Igneous
Metamorphic

GOOD AND BAD

Virtues:	Sins:
Prudence	Pride (or vanity)
Justice	Greed (or avarice)
Temperance	Lust
Courage (or fortitude)	Envy
Faith	Gluttony
Hope	Anger (or wrath)
Charity	Sloth

THE DEITIES OF ANCIENT EGYPT

A. Amun

B. Ra

C. Bastet

D. Isis

E. Osiris

F. Thoth

G. Horus

H. Anubis

TRIVIAL PURSUITS

Subject	Colour
Arts & Literature	Brown
Entertainment	Pink
Geography	Blue
History	Yellow
Science & Nature	Green
Sports & Leisure	Orange

HEAD IN THE CLOUDS

A. Cirrus

B. Cirrocumulus

C. Altocumulus

D. Altostratus

E. Stratus

F. Cumulus

G. Stratuscumulus

H. Cumulonimbus

BUDDHIST TRUTHS

1. Dukkha (the truth of suffering)
2. Samudāya (the truth of the origin of suffering)
3. Nirodha (the truth of the end of suffering)

4. Magga (the truth of the path that leads to the end of suffering)

POEMS (NOT) BY WORDSWORTH

'Ode to a Nightingale'
(by John Keats)

HIGHS AND LOWS

Soprano

Mezzo-soprano

Contralto

Countertenor

Tenor

Baritone

Bass

THE LIVES OF THE WIVES

Name	Fate of Marriage	Children
Catherine of Aragon	Annulled	Henry and Mary
Anne Boleyn	Annulled two days before beheading	Elizabeth
Jane Seymour	Ended with Seymour's death following childbirth	Edward
Anne of Cleves	Annulled	None
Catherine Howard	Ended with beheading	None
Catherine Parr	Ended with Henry's death	None

DINOSAURS PART II

A. *Brachiosaurus*
B. *Dimetrodon*
C. *Diplodocus*
D. *Gallimimus*
E. *Ichthyosaurus*
F. *Parasaurolophus*

SPACE RACE

A. *Sputnik 2* (Laika)
B. *Mercury-Redstone 2* (Ham)
C. *Vladivostok 1* (Yuri Gagarin)
D. *Freedom 7* (Alan Shepard)
E. *Vladivostok 6* (Valentina Tereshkova)
F. *Voskhod 2* (Alexei Leonov)
G. *Apollo 11* (Neil Armstrong; Buzz Aldrin followed him on to the moon, while Michael Collins remained in the command module)

EUROVISION CHAMPS

A. Luxembourg
B. Monaco
C. Netherlands
D. Israel
E. Norway
F. Switzerland
G. Ireland
H. Latvia
I. Ukraine
J. Austria
K. Finland

IF THE SHOE FITS

A. Brogues
B. Chelsea boots
C. Derby
D. Desert boots
E. Monks
F. Oxford

THE PILLARS OF ISLAM

Shahadah (testimony of faith)
Salat (prayer)
Zakat (alms)
Sawm (fasting during the
    month of Ramadan)
Hajj (pilgrimage to Mecca)

NAME THAT ARTIST PART II

A. *Three Tahitian Women*
    by Paul Gauguin
B. *Woman with a Parasol*
    by Claude Monet
C. *The Lake of Zug*
    by J. M. W. Turner
D. *Still Life with Apples and Pears*
    by Paul Cezanne
E. *The Dance Class*
    by Edgar Degas

SPORTING FIGURES

13 (5 + 8)

AYE, AYE CAP'N!

A. *Argo*
B. HMS *Bounty*
C. HMS *Endeavour*
D. *Golden Hind*
E. *Pequod*
F. *Queen Anne's Revenge*
G. HMS *Victory*

LAYERS OF THE EARTH

Crust

Upper Mantle

Lower Mantle

Outer Core

Inner Core

BETTER THAN THE ORIGINAL?

A. *Catch-22*
B. *The Hundred and One Dalmatians*
C. *Little Women*
D. *Trainspotting*
E. *To Kill a Mockingbird*
F. *Twenty Thousand Leagues Under the Sea*
G. *The Godfather*
H. *The Three Musketeers*

THE COUNTRY FORMERLY KNOWN AS ...

Swaziland

THROWING A GOOGLY

1. Wicketkeeper
2. Slips
3. Gully
4. Point
5. Cover
6. Third man
7. Fine leg
8. Midwicket
9. Mid-off
10. Square leg

THE MOVIES OF JOHN GRISHAM

A Time to Kill
The Chamber
The Client
The Firm
The Pelican Brief
The Rainmaker
Runaway Jury

POKER FACE

High card
Pair
Two pairs
Three of a kind
Straight
Flush
Full house
Four of a kind
Straight flush
Royal flush

SUPER BOWL

Players:
Tom Brady (7 rings)
Charles Haley (5)

Player and coach:
Bill Belichick

OCEAN'S 11

A. George Clooney
B. Bernie Mac
C. Brad Pitt
D. Elliott Gould
E. Casey Affleck
F. Scott Caan
G. Eddie Jemison
H. Don Cheadle
I. Shaobo Qin
J. Carl Reiner
K. Matt Damon

WHAT GOES AROUND COMES AROUND

Limbo
Lust
Gluttony
Greed
Wrath (or anger)
Heresy
Violence
Fraud
Treachery

GROUP THINK

A. Coalition
B. Intrusion
C. Parliament
D. Shrewdness
E. Crash
F. Prickle
G. Pod
H. Bloat

A HERCULEAN CHALLENGE

The Nemean Lion
The Lernaean Hydra
The Ceryneian Hind
The Erymanthian Boar
The Augean Stables
The Stymphalian Birds
The Cretan Bull

The Mares of Diomedes
The Belt of Hippolyta
The Cattle of Geryon
The Golden Apples of the
    Hesperides
Cerberus

E. Poland
F. Italy
G. Malaysia
H. India
I. South Africa
J. Australia
K. Spain
L. Nigeria

WHAT DO YOU SEE?

Artist: Canaletto

Location: The Square of Saint Mark's, Venice

THREE WISE MEN

Melchior (Persia)
Caspar (India)
Balthazar (Arabia)

POLITICAL NUMBER-CRUNCHING

40 (27 + 13)

GREAT LAKE STATES

Illinois
Indiana
Michigan
Minnesota
New York
Ohio
Pennsylvania
Wisconsin

A PLACE CALLED HOME

A. Brazil
B. Canada
C. Colombia
D. Japan

JOIN THE DOTS

Albert Einstein

THE NOVELS OF GEORGE R. R. MARTIN

A Game of Thrones
A Clash of Kings
A Storm of Swords
A Feast for Crows
A Dance with Dragons
The Winds of Winter
A Dream of Spring

SPORTS OF CHAMPIONS

A. Squash
B. Skiing
C. Figure skating
D. Badminton
E. Darts
F. Triathlon
G. Speed skating
H. Swimming
I. Crown green bowling

RUB-A-DUB-DUB

The butcher, the baker
and the candlestick maker

BEST ACTORS NEVER TO HAVE WON AN OSCAR

Tom Cruise and Glenn Close

CLASSICAL ARCHITECTURE

A. Tuscan
B. Doric
C. Ionic
D. Corinthian
E. Composite

MOTOWN

A. Marvin Gaye and Tammi Terrell
B. The Temptations
C. Jimmy Ruffin
D. Stevie Wonder
E. Mary Wells
F. The Elgins
G. Diana Ross and The Supremes
H. Boyz II Men
I. Bobby Taylor and The Vancouvers
J. The Marvelettes

THE PENTATEUCH

Genesis

Exodus

Leviticus

Numbers

Deuteronomy

THE WORLD OF WINE

A. Chile

B. USA

C. China

D. Australia

E. Italy

F. New Zealand

G. Spain

H. UK

I. Portugal

J. Hungary

K. Germany

L. Russia

M. South Africa

N. Georgia

WORDS AND NUMBERS

154 (7 x 22)

TURNING OVER A NEW LEAF

A. Oak

B. Chestnut

C. Ash

D. Birch   E. Cedar

F. Beech   G. Pine

FAMOUS LAST WORDS PART II

A. *The Unbearable Lightness of Being* (Milan Kundera)
B. *Crime and Punishment* (Fyodor Dostoyevsky)
C. *The Book Thief* (Markus Zusak)
D. *The Handmaid's Tale* (Margaret Atwood)
E. *The Stranger* (Albert Camus)
F. *Wuthering Heights* (Emily Brontë)
G. *Adventures of Huckleberry Finn* (Mark Twain)
H. *A Portrait of the Artist as a Young Man* (James Joyce)
I. *Slaughterhouse-Five* (Kurt Vonnegut)

THE AVENGERS

Ant-Man
The Hulk
Iron Man
Thor
The Wasp

SAY WHEN

A. 1903
B. 1912
C. 1928
D. 1933
E. 1947
F. 1954
G. 1968
H. 1974
I. 1981
J. 1998

RAINBOW NATION

Black, blue, green, red, white and yellow

THE MODERN PENTATHLON

Épée fencing
Freestyle swimming
Show jumping
Pistol shooting
Cross-country running

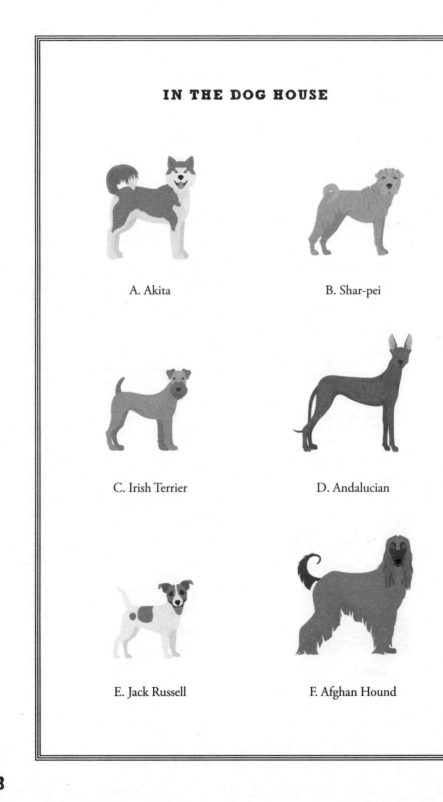

IN THE DOG HOUSE

A. Akita

B. Shar-pei

C. Irish Terrier

D. Andalucian

E. Jack Russell

F. Afghan Hound

G. Bichon-frise

H. Schnauzer

I. Boxer

J. Labrador

K. Corgi

L. Pomeranian

WIMBLEDON WINNERS

Monica Seles and
Ken Rosewall

MONOPOLY!

Go
Free Parking
Go to Jail
Just Visiting

THE CITIES OF IRELAND

1. Dublin
2. Cork
3. Galway
4. Limerick
5. Waterford

FEELING THE HEAT

Conduction, Convection, Radiation

GENERAL KNOWLEDGE WORDSEARCH

A. *Casino Royale*

B. Duke Ellington

C. St Petersburg

D. Raphael

E. Emmental

F. Lord Byron

G. Suleiman

H. Ashgabat

I. Merengue

J. David Hockney

K. Sergey Bubka

L. Gettysburg

M. Cicero

N. Nikola Tesla

O. Hugo Chavez

P. Le Corbusier

L	T	K	N	S	N	X	W	O	E	D	K	V	X	R	Q	W	X	S	Z	R	C	Q
O	L	E	A	H	P	A	R	V	Y	E	N	K	C	O	H	D	I	V	A	D	M	H
A	N	Z	D	B	H	F	M	E	R	E	N	G	U	E	M	K	Z	A	Q	O	L	E
C	M	S	V	U	I	O	X	R	N	L	D	X	X	A	B	L	J	G	Z	M	F	C
A	Y	E	T	A	K	N	X	S	C	X	G	E	T	T	Y	S	B	U	R	G	N	S
S	K	R	G	A	C	E	I	F	C	K	C	F	C	L	G	D	B	N	M	I	L	Y
I	O	G	N	D	S	V	E	K	e	R	E	I	S	U	B	R	O	C	B	S	M	Z
N	Q	E	O	Z	I	H	V	L	O	U	B	M	T	G	Y	S	J	F	D	U	U	E
O	A	I	R	Z	K	T	G	G	L	L	U	E	L	C	F	J	N	M	V	L	P	V
R	P	B	Y	E	O	Y	C	A	Z	I	A	M	O	A	D	K	F	W	V	E	W	A
O	W	U	B	R	T	J	J	P	B	B	N	T	E	J	T	Z	O	C	C	I	Q	H
Y	D	B	D	Y	X	E	Q	R	N	A	K	G	E	X	G	N	V	T	I	M	Y	C
A	G	K	R	C	K	L	T	R	F	G	T	B	T	S	L	H	E	X	V	A	F	O
L	V	A	O	X	C	I	C	E	R	O	L	J	W	O	L	I	Z	M	J	N	C	G
E	K	K	L	I	T	L	Z	W	Q	H	I	U	M	S	N	A	X	U	M	V	N	U
M	C	D	O	G	R	U	B	S	R	E	T	E	P	T	S	F	R	E	S	E	G	H

BRITISH PRIME MINISTERS

1. Sir Robert Walpole
(20 years, 314 days)

2. William Pitt the Younger
(18 years, 343 days)

3. The Earl of Liverpool
(14 years, 305 days)

4. The Marquess of Salisbury
(13 years, 252 days)

5. William Gladstone
(12 years, 126 days)

6. Lord North
(12 years, 58 days)

7. Margaret Thatcher
(11 years, 208 days)

8. Henry Pelham
(10 years, 191 days)

9. Tony Blair
(10 years, 56 days)

10. Viscount Palmerston
(9 years, 141 days)

ALL ABOARD THE ARK

Shem
Ham
Japheth

THE EARTH'S ATMOSPHERE

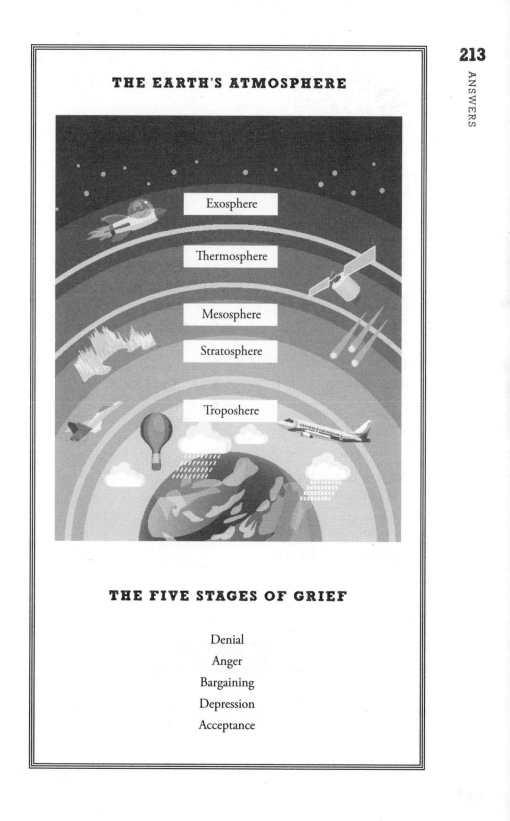

Exosphere

Thermosphere

Mesosphere

Stratosphere

Troposhere

THE FIVE STAGES OF GRIEF

Denial

Anger

Bargaining

Depression

Acceptance

IN THE WORDS OF POTUS PART II

A. Ronald Reagan
B. Harry S. Truman
C. Richard Nixon
D. George H. W. Bush
E. Barack Obama
F. Theodore Roosevelt

RIVERS OF HADES

Acheron (river of woe)
Cocytus (river of lamentation)
Phlegethon (river of fire)
Styx (river of unbreakable oath)
Lethe (river of forgetfulness)

PAR FOR THE COURSE

Carnoustie Golf Links, Muirfield, Old Course at St Andrews, Royal St George's Golf Club, Royal Liverpool Golf Club, Royal Troon Golf Club, Royal Lytham & St Annes Golf Club, Royal Portrush Golf Club, Royal Birkdale Golf Club and Turnberry

FOUR HORSEMEN

Death, Famine, Conquest (or Pestilence) and War

STAR OF NOIR

The Big Sleep
Farewell, My Lovely
The High Window
The Lady in the Lake
The Little Sister
The Long Good-bye
Playback

A WHALE OF A TIME

Blue whale
Fin whale
Bowhead whale
Right whale
Sperm whale
Humpback whale

HARRISON FORD MOVIES

Cape Fear
Schindler's List

THE NEED FOR SPEED

Lewis Hamilton (95)

Michael Schumacher (91)

Sebastian Vettel (53)

Alain Prost (51)

Ayrton Senna (41)

Fernando Alonso (32)

Nigel Mansell (31)

BY A NECK

Poethlyn (1918 and 1919)

Reynoldstown (1935 and 1936)

Red Rum (1973, 1974 and 1977)

Tiger Roll (2018 and 2019)

BOURNE READY

The Bourne Identity, The Bourne Supremacy, The Bourne Ultimatum The Bourne Legacy, Jason Bourne

A RIGHT RACKET

Women

Serena Williams (23)

Steffi Graf (22)

Chris Evert (18)

Martina Navratilova (18)

Margaret Court (11)

Monica Seles (9)

Billie Jean King (8)

Evonne Goolagong (7)

Justine Henin (7)

Venus Williams (7)

Martina Hingis (5)

Maria Sharapova (5)

Men

Roger Federer (20)

Rafael Nadal (20)

Novak Djokovic (17)

Pete Sampras (14)

Björn Borg (11)

Jimmy Connors (8)

Ivan Lendl (8)

Andre Agassi (8)

John McEnroe (7)

Mats Wilander (7)

Stefan Edberg (6)

Boris Becker (6)

Rod Laver (5)

John Newcombe (5)

WE THREE KINGS

George V

Edward VIII

George VI

APING AROUND

Bonobos

Chimpanzees

Gorillas

Humans

Orangutans

AND CUT!

Alice Doesn't Live Here Anymore

Raging Bull

The Color of Money

Goodfellas

The Age of Innocence

The Aviator

The Departed

Hugo

SWEEPING THE OSCARS

It Happened One Night

One Flew Over the Cuckoo's Nest

The Silence of the Lambs

THE STONE AGE

Paleolithic

Mesolithic

Neolithic

LITTLE WOMEN

Meg, Jo, Beth and Amy

AUSTRALIAN STATES AND THEIR CAPITALS

State/Territory	Capital
Australian Capital Territory	Canberra
New South Wales	Sydney
Northern Territory	Darwin
Queensland	Brisbane
South Australia	Adelaide
Tasmania	Hobart
Victoria	Melbourne
Western Australia	Perth

THE WOMEN OF SEX AND THE CITY

Carrie Bradshaw (played by
   Sarah Jessica Parker)
Samantha Jones (Kim Cattrall)
Miranda Hobbes (Cynthia Nixon)
Charlotte York (Kristin Davis)

A CHALLENGE TOO FAR?

Michael Ballack
Roberto Baggio

WORLD MUSIC

South Korea
Brazil
Jamaica

THE POETRY OF A. A. MILNE

When We Were Very Young and
Now We Are Six

THE WORKS OF GEORGE ELLIOT

Adam Bede
The Mill on the Floss
Silas Marner
Romola
Felix Holt, the Radical
Middlemarch
Daniel Deronda

BORN TO BE WILDE

Vera; or, The Nihilists
The Duchess of Padua
Lady Windermere's Fan
A Woman of No Importance
Salomé
An Ideal Husband
The Importance of Being Earnest

E = MC²

E = Energy
m = mass
c = the speed of light

THE NOVELS OF UMBERTO ECO

The Name of the Rose
Foucault's Pendulum
The Island of the Day Before
Baudolino
*The Mysterious Flame of
    Queen Loana*
The Prague Cemetery
Numero Zero

THREE MEN AND A BABY

Ted Danson
Steve Guttenberg
Tom Selleck

FRESH AIR

Nitrogen
Oxygen
Carbon dioxide
Argon
Neon
Helium
Methane

GASSING AWAY

Argon
Chlorine
Fluorine
Helium
Hydrogen
Krypton
Neon
Nitrogen
Oxygen
Radon
Xenon

A COUNTRY APART

Fiji

PAW PATROL

Ryder
Chase
Marshall
Rocky
Rubble
Skye
Zuma

DARLING CHILDREN

Wendy

John

Michael

ALL IN THE EYES

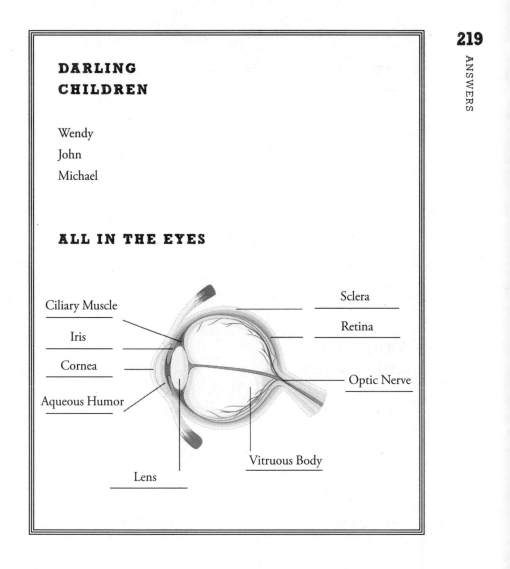

Ciliary Muscle

Iris

Cornea

Aqueous Humor

Lens

Sclera

Retina

Optic Nerve

Vitruous Body

NOTES

NOTES

NOTES

NOTES

NOTES